LUNAR MAGIC

A BEGINNER'S GUIDE TO LIVING AND WORKING WITH MOON CYCLES AND PHASES

ASHLEY BRITTANY

Published by *Master Plan Focus.*

Contents

Dedication

To the luminous glow of the Moon that whispers secrets through the night, this book is dedicated to my celestial guide and Mother, whose love and wisdom have always been my guiding light. Your faith in my journey has made all the difference, illuminating paths I only dared to dream of.

And to the wanderers of the night sky, my readers, who have joined me in uncovering the mysteries held by the stars and now, the enchanting Moon. Your passion and curiosity fuel the magic of this journey. May the Moon's phases remind you of life's constant ebb and flow, encouraging you to embrace change with grace and to find magic in the everyday.

May our nights be blessed with clarity and our hearts with courage as we navigate the tides of destiny under the Moon's watchful gaze.

With love and lunar light,
Ashley x

Your FREE E-Book: Full & New Moon Rituals

Please download and enjoy your FREE Full & New Moon Rituals guide, which will wonderfully complement the book that you are about to read!

Scan the QR code below to access your download.

Your FREE Journal: Master Your Moon Manifestation

Nourish your new-found love for our Moon and its wonderful manifestation power with your FREE journal download.

Scan the QR code below to access your free download. Feel free to print it out, as many times as you like, or save and edit the document within your devices if you prefer to harness the power of technology!

INTRODUCTION

You are standing outside, barefoot on a warm summer's night with the soft grass between your toes. As you look to the horizon, you see a shining light begin to rise over the ocean; the moment you have been waiting for. The Full Moon will light up the sky tonight, drawing you into its mystery. Inviting you into a place of curiosity, where the lunar rays will open your heart and mind to answers that have been residing within you.

How do you feel when you gaze at the Moon?

Do you wait for its arrival each month so that you can dance under its rays?

Before you begin this book, think about how the Moon has influenced you in the past. Think about what made you pick up this book and read about the ancient wisdom that it holds.

There is an abundance of history, mythology, and science connected with the Moon in our sky, and we are going to explore it all throughout the following pages.

Back to the Beginning:

Let's start way back in ancient times when our ancestors who walked this Earth would use the Moon as a guiding light. The extra light of a Full Moon would provide an extra chance to hunt during the night, securing their food source for the tribe and moving in the cool weather as a respite to the summer heat. Before our modern technology existed, ancient cultures were well-versed in moon phases and connected with the energetic cycles of the Moon. They depended on the Moon just as they depended on their next breath. From cave paintings of the Moon's cycles to rituals and rites of passage performed during specific times in a Moon phase, the rhythm of the Moon is one that has been followed since ancient times.

What is so Special about the Moon?

There is no doubt that the Moon holds a specific feel and that it influences the world around us. The Moon has been worshipped as a God in some cultures and religions. Its energy is used for healing in witchcraft and nature-based therapies. You just need to look over the fence to see your neighbor dancing wild and naked under the moonlight to know that the Moon brings out the crazy, wild, and authentic side of everyone.

So let's zoom into the power of the Moon. Moon phases and their energies are a sub-section in Western Astrology. It is one celestial body that exerts an effect on Earth, and although it creates a strong effect alone, it should also be considered in its role in the greater scheme of Astrology.

If you want to go back to the basics and beginnings, my first book 'Astrology for Beginners' is a great place to start. The book provides an in-depth overview of all the aspects of Western Astrology and will teach you how to find your sun, rising, and moon signs.

The Moon is the emotional part of your personality. Your moon sign will have a specific and personal effect on your life and the way you deal with and process your emotions.

If you have ever felt agitated for no apparent reason, or experienced a sleepless night, only to look up and notice a Full Moon shining in the sky, then you know first-hand how strong the effects of the Moon can be. Whether the Moon is bringing too much or too little energy into our bodies is influenced directly by the phase that the Moon is in. The lunar energy is like a current of electricity that runs through the physical body. Although it's an unseen force, it is powerful beyond measure.

Breaking Down the Book:

Throughout this book, we will look at the Moon from a more general perspective.

We will explore the feelings that it draws out of us each month, as it is strongly connected to the movement of water and energy on our planet.

After reading this book, you will understand how to read and interpret the lunar energy and lunar phases. You will also know how to apply the energy of the zodiac signs to the current lunar phase and experience an even deeper connection with the lunar cycles.

In this book, the Moon's cycles will be introduced as well as some examples of the ways that the Moon influences everyday life.

Chapter One will explore the evidence of the connection between the Earth and the sky. There are some real-life examples of tidal changes, animal habits, and human statistics that prove the Moon's magnetism and effect on our planet.

In Chapter Two, you will start to discover what each different phase of the Moon represents. You'll find an in-depth explanation of each phase, and you'll be able to apply it to your own life.

Moving into Chapters Three and Four, the information about a New Moon takes a deep dive. If you ever wonder about what to do or not to do during a New Moon transit, these chapters have the answers. There are also twelve rituals for each of the Zodiac signs. You are invited to connect with the energy of these rituals to develop your own sense of inner knowing or intuition about Moon energy.

Chapters Five and Six are focused on the Full Moon and you'll find another twelve Moon rituals there too. This time, the energy is expressive and outgoing, shining light on previously hidden parts of your life.

Chapter Seven takes you through the basics of how to apply these rituals, and to create both short-term and long-term goals in alignment with the Moon phases to enhance your manifestation abilities. Everyone has the potential of manifestation within them (this, I do truly believe) and by synchronizing this ability with the supportive energy of the Moon, you may just find your life changing quickly before your eyes.

The final chapter is one last little surprise. There you will explore a number of 'special' Moon phases, including Super Moons, Micro Moons, and eclipses. You'll gain a new understanding of how to use this amplified energy in accordance with the lunar cycles.

How to Use this Book:

Considering the above information, I have a few tips on how to get the most out of the book:

- Read through the introduction and Chapters One and Two thoroughly, absorbing the information as you go.

- Take a yearly calendar or diary, and using a Moon calculator from the internet, mark both the New and Full Moons on your calendar. If you see that it's a supermoon or eclipse you can mark this information too.

- In regard to the calendar idea above, with a little research, you may find that a local astrologer from your area has created a specific Moon diary. This should provide you with the relevant Moon times, according to your time zone.

- On the first New Moon, read through Chapters Three and Four, taking part in the relevant ritual.

- If you find that a Full Moon is coming up first, then read through Chapters Five and Six during the Full Moon transit.

- You don't need to read through all the rituals at once; you can simply choose the relevant ritual for the Zodiac sign and return to the next ritual on the following New or Full Moon!

- Be sure to read Chapters Seven and Eight, digesting that information as it feels right for you.

- Be kind to yourself while learning! There is a lot of information in this book, so take it easy as you let it soak in.

Applying one new ritual, idea, or inspiration each month will create a sustainable path to eventually integrate all of the Moon's wisdom into your life.

The Importance of Rituals:

The reason you will find so many rituals in this book is due to the energy that they create. When you take part in a ritual, whether by yourself or with a group, the idea is to tune into a different energy. To shift your energy body from one way of being to another. If you sync this up with the energy of the Moon, not only do you shift your energy, but you also connect to a deeper energetic force that is running through the entire Universe.

Connect to this energy frequently by moon gazing and listening to how your body reacts to the phases of the Moon, and you will soon see your life change in a positive and profound way.

A Final Reminder:

If you are reading this now, know that you are here for a reason. The unseen but deeply felt forces of the Moon are beckoning you to move closer to the wisdom that is held in the phases.

As you learn about the energetic world of the Moon, you will remember the origins of your soul. You are made of the same stardust and atoms that make up the magnificent Moon. You are an extension of the Universe itself. The pull that you feel on the Full Moon, and the intuitive call you hear on the New Moon is your own true nature syncing with the nature of the entire solar system.

<u>CHAPTER 1</u>

THE CONNECTION BETWEEN EARTH AND SKY

It's easy to dismiss the Moon's influence on Earth as mere myth, magic, or mystery, but when the evidence stacks up, you might just be surprised at how much we are actually affected by the lunar energy.

Perhaps you have found this book because you are interested in finding out why you feel a little crazy on the Full Moon, or why your energy changes each month in rhythm with the Moon. If you think about it, the word lunatic is derived from 'lunar' which by definition means 'determined by the Moon'. So, it is no wonder that these cycles are affecting you and every other human on this planet.

Evidence of the Moon's phases and their Earthly influence started many moons ago with elders telling stories around a campfire and old folklore stories being shared amongst tribes. Fast forward to today, with progressive technology and access to many people, cultures, and events around the world, it is becoming more and more evident that the Moon is influencing human (and animal) reactions. Let's explore what this looks like.

<u>Sleep Studies and the Moon:</u>

One of the most common complaints about the Full Moon is the lack of sleep that people get. A study from 2013 showed that people spent less time in NREM sleep (deep sleep) and slept for twenty minutes less during a Full Moon when compared to other times of the month. This study was measured under the highly controlled conditions of a circadian laboratory study, which confirms the effects of lunar energy on sleep cycles (1).

One of the theories about less sleep on the Full Moon is that our ancestors probably stayed up later and got more work done when there was more natural light available in the sky – i.e., the time of the Full Moon. This exposure to extra natural light can affect melatonin production, the natural sleep hormone in the body. The amount of melatonin in your body is directly related to the amount of light around you. Melatonin is produced in the lead-up to bedtime, as your surrounding environment starts to become darker. Then, when morning comes, melatonin production comes to a stop as the eyes are exposed to light – whether that's sunlight, moonlight, or artificial light.

This could be why the extra lunar light delays the onset of melatonin production and therefore delays the onset of sleep on Full Moon evenings. Although this is a strong idea, some studies have shown that the Moon's effect is due to more than just the light in the sky.

A sleep study from 2021 compared people from the city of Seattle (who are more exposed to artificial lights) with those living in indigenous communities in rural environments in Argentina. The study showed that both groups of people slept less in the lead-up to the Full Moon. In cities such as Seattle, you can expect that the moonlight is overpowered by streetlights, car headlights, and lit-up signs. This indicates that the lunar power affecting sleep levels can be attributed to more than just its bright light. Comparing two different groups shows us that regardless of access to electricity and artificial light sources, there is an innate adaptation that makes us sleep less during the Full Moon (2).

Increased Accidents During a Full Moon:

Lack of sleep has a lot of effects on the body and mind, and it can be attributed to slower reaction times, taking more risks, and therefore creating more accidents. If the whole world is sleeping less during the time of the Full Moon, it could be easy to suggest the correlation between the Full Moon and increased accident rates.

A study that ran over 40 years to understand the effect of the Full Moon on motorcyclist deaths revealed a 5% increase in the chance of a fatal motorcycle accident on Full Moon nights compared to ones without a Full Moon. Supermoons were shown to be even worse for safety, increasing the likelihood by 32% (3).

With 40 years of evidence, it's wise to advise extra safety precautions around the time of the Full Moon, whether you are driving or not.

We Are Made of Water:

Made up of around 55-78% water, the Moon pulls on our gravitational forces. This could be one reason that we feel more scattered, energized, or wired under the Full Moon because many forces are at play, pulling our attention in multiple directions.

It doesn't take much to connect our watery bodies with the movement of the Moon. Although it may feel small to us, you can witness the huge power of the Moon on bigger bodies of water around our planet. One of the most visible ways to see the impact of the Moon on the Earth is through looking at ocean tides. Tides are the way the water moves in and out, as if moving energetically. This big movement of water happens because of the gravitational pull between the Moon and the Earth. Both the Earth and the Moon have a gravity of their own. Although the Moon's gravitational pull is weaker than the one on Earth, it still affects the liquid water on the Earth's surfaces. As these two orbiting forces move around one another, the Moon draws the liquid water in parts of the Earth to a bulge (a high tide), while the lesser influenced parts are reduced to a low tide. As the Moon moves, the influence is changed, creating different tides during different times of the day.

One of the biggest tides in the world can be seen in the Bay of Fundy in Canada. In this special location, the tidal difference is up to thirteen meters. At the head of the bay, the tide can rise and drop sixteen meters, which is the height of a four-story building (4). Now that's a pretty big influence!

Animal Habits in Sync with Moon Cycles:

If the Moon can impact the ocean, why wouldn't it impact our systems too? Not only us but all of life on Earth. There are certain species of animals both on land and in the ocean that have adapted their biological rhythms to tune in with the Moon.

In the ocean, many species of tropical corals spawn (releasing eggs and sperm for reproduction) during the night of the Full Moon. There has also been evidence of annelid worms floating to the ocean surface during waxing Moons, always in tune with the lunar cycles.

As humans, with watches, calendars, and many ways to track time, we have created an artificial system that we follow to keep our plans and meet our friends. This system is known as the Gregorian Calendar year and it works in a pattern of months and years. But without the need for watches, the only unchanging rhythms in nature are the solar patterns of night and day, the seasons, and the lunar cycle. These are the natural patterns that animal life is attuned to on a biological level.

Various types of sea turtles would be lost if the Moon were to disappear. These species have evolved with the movement of the ocean and are highly attuned to the rising and falling tides. They lay their eggs in the sand and time their hatching to coincide with the tides that will give their offspring the best possible chance of survival. Without the Moon to guide the tides, the turtles would have a very slim chance of making it into the water alive.

Regarding land animals, small mammals in Australia have been shown to increase their night activity on darker evenings, when there is less light in the sky. This activity around the time of the New Moon, helps to protect them from being prey to larger animals, but also provides an important window of time to find food.

Birds on the other hand are sometimes more active at night, differing their activity on the night of a Full Moon compared to a New Moon. A specific example is the male willy wagtail birds that sing the most on the night of a Full Moon. If only we knew what they were singing about!

Menstruation and the Moon

Another aspect of the human body syncing with the lunar cycles can be seen when you look at the menstrual cycle. In some cultures or traditions, the menstrual cycle is even called a 'moon cycle' as both the Moon's cycle and the menstrual cycle are deeply connected with emotional expression. Connected with the hormones, there is a set time of New Moon energy during the bleed, that invites the body to move slowly and be gentle. Then, there is the yang part of the cycle during ovulation, when the body is invited to express itself out into the world.

Another similarity in these two events is that the average length of a menstrual cycle is also around 29 days, the same as a lunar cycle. Surely this is no coincidence.

If you are a menstruator, notice if your cycle is synced with the Moon. If it is now, perhaps by engaging in rituals and moongazing more frequently, the body will return to its natural rhythms guided by lunar light.

One of the biggest obstacles to syncing with the Moon relates to the amount of artificial light, electronic devices, and magnetic items in our immediate environment. Therefore, if you truly want to sync up with nature, try spending some evenings gazing at the stars while barefoot on the beach or in a forest! It will give you a much more pure connection without distraction from other electrical interference.

What Would Happen if the Moon Disappeared?

Seeing that the Moon has an impact on humans, animals, sea life, and ocean tides, what would happen if this lunar force was taken out of orbit?

If the Moon was to disappear, the biggest impact would be on Earth's rotational balance. Today, the axis of Earth is titled specifically in connection with Earth's orbit around the sun. If the Moon were to go, the Earth would have a wobble in its spin cycle, potentially throwing everything off balance (5).

Not only would our Earth become unpredictable and shaky, but imagine a world with no tides rising or falling, and no evenings spent under the glow of the Full Moon. The stars might seem brighter, but there would be a big glow missing from our sky, taking away the magical experience of moon-bathing.

Notice the Moon's Influence:

When you look up at the sky each night, it is easy to observe where the Moon is and what phase it is in. The phases change from night to night, moving in rhythmical cycles.

Every change that happens on any level, creates a reaction. This is true for small changes you may make in your life, for example: getting a haircut creates a new feeling in yourself, or challenging yourself to go to a new event creates new connections in your life. There are also bigger changes that you can make that will have bigger influences, such as deciding to change jobs or careers which will then change the trajectory of your life, or moving to a new city or country that will encourage you to step out of your comfort zone. Whether small or large, these kinds of changes are being encouraged by the Moon each month so that we are in a cycle of growth, moving forward, and creating a new reality.

The more connected you become to the phases and changes, the more observant you will be to see these changes happening in your life.

As you work through this book, start to think about the changes that occur each month. You can reflect on the following questions to get started:

1. Do your energy levels change throughout the month? When do you feel energised and when do you feel exhausted?

2. Have you noticed any small occurrences or accidents that hap-

pen around a full or New Moon? Could you put these down with a date to reflect on in comparison to the Moon cycles?

3. At what phases of the Moon do you feel more emotional, extroverted, introverted, or calm? Notice if these emotional states correlate to the New and Full Moon times.

The more you listen to your inner guidance, the clearer the connection between yourself and the Moon will be. Then, once this connection is clear, you will no longer question why you want to go inwards and be by yourself at certain times of the month, but instead, you will embrace these times with open arms, knowing that they are important moments of potential and growth.

How to Connect With the Moon:

Start now: get curious about how the Moon talks with you. This evening, head outside and try to spot the Moon in the sky. Get to know where it rises and where it sets (which will differ slightly each evening). Try to work out what phase it is in and listen to what it is trying to tell you.

If you do spot the Moon, take three deep and nourishing breaths, inviting the moonlight into your body with every inhale, and grounding that energy down into your body on each exhale. Let the moonlight wash over you and enjoy its essence. If you open up and invite the Moon in to be your friend, you might just be surprised how willing it is to share its energy with you.

Go forward through this book with an open mind, a feeling of curiosity, and a sense of adventure. There is lunar magic waiting to connect with you!

References:

1. Cajochen, C., Altanay-Ekici, S., Münch, M., Frey, S., Knoblauch, V., & Wirz-Justice, A. (2013). Evidence that the lunar cycle influences human sleep. Current Biology, 23(15), 1485–1488. https://doi.org/10.1016/j.cub.2013.06.029

2. Cho, Y., Ryu, S. H., Lee, B. R., Kim, K. H., Lee, E., & Choi, J. (2015). Effects of artificial light at night on human health: A literature review of observational and experimental studies applied to exposure assessment. Chronobiology international, 32(9), 1294–1310. https://doi.org/10.3109/07420528.2015.1073158

3. Redelmeier, D. A., & Shafir, E. (2017). The full moon and motorcycle related mortality: Population based double control study. BMJ. https://doi.org/10.1136/bmj.j5367

4. Bay of fundy tides: The highest tides in the world!. Bay of Fundy. (2019, June 13). https://www.bayoffundy.com/about/highest-tides/

5. How does the Moon affect the earth? | institute of physics. (2023, September 14). https://www.iop.org/explore-physics/moon/how-does-moon-affect-earth

CHAPTER 2

MOON PHASES: LEARNING ABOUT THE LUNAR CYCLES

Everything in nature moves in cycles, and so too does the Moon.

If you have ever looked up at the sky on a few consecutive nights, you will notice that the Moon is always in a different phase in a different part of the sky. The Moon is always in motion. It rotates around Earth and creates eight distinct phases. So how are the phases created?

The Sun is the only light-producing object in our solar system, giving us the qualities of night and day as Earth rotates around it. The Moon rotates around Earth on its own orbital path and therefore sees different amounts of light from time to time.

When the Moon is moving in the space between Earth and the Sun, we see a 'New Moon' in the sky. This creates an invisible Moon as from our perspective, we only see the dark side of the Moon.

From here, the Moon continues its journey, moving through waxing crescent, first quarter, and waxing gibbous phases before becoming fully illuminated in the sky.

Full illumination is the time of the Full Moon when the Moon is on the opposite side of Earth to the Sun. This sunlight that reaches the face of the Moon creates a bright reflection, showing us one full half of the Moon's surface (to us on Earth, this looks like the Moon is fully illuminated).

After the Full Moon comes waning gibbous, last quarter, and waxing gibbous phases before the New Moon arrives again, starting a new cycle.

The scientific explanation of the Moon is easy to observe if you watch the sky during the night (or sometimes the day). Every night there will be a slight change in the light that reflects on the Moon's surface, and as you track this change, you will be able to tell which phase the Moon is in.

One full lunar cycle is twenty-nine and a half days long, meaning that the New Moon will occur every twenty-nine & a half days. This brings rhythm and method to the Moon's movement, allowing us to rely on the predictability of the lunar cycles.

So, you now understand how the physical movement of the Moon, Sun, and Earth create the Moon's cycles, but how about the energetic influences of the Moon?

The Energy of the Moon

Energetically, the Moon is the ruler of emotions. It is the planet that is associated with the 'Mother' archetype and femininity, due to its tendency to express its emotional needs clearly and publicly.

If you were to personify the Moon, it would be a sensitive and caring person, one who is unafraid to look at the nature of its own being, whilst being able to set reasonable boundaries to protect itself from the energetic attack of others.

Wherever the Moon is found on your astrological birth chart will indicate how you can best express and process your emotions. It also gives you insight into how and where you can make yourself feel most comfortable and most at home! The term 'home' could refer to a specific place in the world, but it could also be the notion of creating a home within yourself.

Above all, the Moon is a planet that will invite you to go deeper into your feeling state, to get to know your energetic body, and to listen to the energetic pull of the Universe around you.

The Energetic Expression of the Eight Moon Phases

As different amounts of light hit the Moon's surface and the phases change, so does the amount of lunar energy shining down here on Earth. This affects our body, mind, and mood, as well as the energy of the world around us. When you get to know and understand the energy of each phase, you can use this to your advantage.

Every new cycle is a new beginning, a chance to start fresh and to grow in a new direction. In a calendar year, we usually have twelve (occasionally thirteen) New Moon cycles. This provides you with at least twelve chances for reflection and resetting the course of your life. Let's take a look at how you can do that.

For a visual (and more Earthly) representation, the energy of the Moon phases can be compared to planting a seed and watching it grow. The New Moon is a new seed, planted in the earth. Then as it grows, every cycle is a chance to shed dead leaves and old flowers, so that the fresh energy can be channelled into new growth in the next phase. Little by little, growth continues, shaping the plant in new and unusual ways as it grows toward its biggest and brightest expression.

Now imagine that you are the plant, and the seed is an intention that you plant within your heart. Moving with the Moon cycles is one way that you can alter the course of your life. If you consciously bring the practice of following the Moon cycles into your awareness, you will be the one writing your own story and forging the path that you want to walk.

As you read through the following phases, contemplate how the energy of each phase fits into your life. To help you with this contemplation, you can use the reflection question at the end of each phase. You can think about them in your mind, or record your answers in a journal.

New Moon – New Beginnings

The darkest and most invisible phase of the Moon is the New Moon. This is a time of introspection, an invitation to go deep within yourself and to listen to your inner voice of intuition.

In the seed cycle, this is the time to plant the seed. All seeds start in darkness, covered by earth, deep in the soil. This darkness is the incubator for ideas and expressions that you wish to cultivate. It's a time spent away from the outside experience of the world, so that you can form ideas of your own, from a place of neutrality, rather than be influenced by what is already in the atmosphere around you.

At the time of the New Moon, think about what you want your next twenty-nine and a half days to look like. What habits do you want to begin? What attitude do you want to have toward life? What skills can you learn or apply to your life?

If you spend time in quiet introspection, you may notice that the answers to these questions arise naturally, almost spontaneously, as you tune into the essence residing at the core of your being.

Once you have planted your seed of intention, you are on your way to a fresh beginning. As the darkness leaves and light begins to shine on the Moon, the journey will continue to unfold.

Reflection Question for the New Moon:

What seed am I planting with my daily actions?

Note: We will explore more about the New Moon in the following chapter. You will also find a number of rituals to help you cultivate your dreams and set your New Moon intentions in Chapter Four.

Waxing Crescent Moon (also known simply as Crescent Moon) – Gaining Momentum

After the darkest hour, the first glimpse of light always seems to shine extra bright. The waxing crescent phase of the Moon can feel like a crescent smile spreading across your face. If you did use the New Moon time to set your intentions, chances are that you are feeling inspired and motivated during this time. This is when your ideas are gaining momentum and starting to take shape.

At this time, the seed that you planted is being watered. The 'water' that you are giving is your energy, your time, your thoughts, and your intention. Take a moment now to think about what will you water your seed with.

When this phase arrives, you might have more clarity about what it takes to bring your dreams into reality or what resources you need to support you on your journey. Reflection moves into action as the path forward makes its way known. Now go and gather up the resources you require so that you can begin working on your intention.

Reflection Question for the Waxing Crescent Moon:

What is inspiring me right now and how can I follow that feeling of inspiration flowing through me?

First Quarter Moon – The Foundations Have Been Set

The First Quarter Moon indicates that you are a quarter of the way through the current moon cycle. By this time, your foundation has (hopefully) been set. If you created an intention for this cycle and stuck to it, then the work you have done leading up to this First Quarter Moon is solidified. You can use this time for reflection and inner inquiry. Think about if you are on track with your goals or if you need to make any changes in the lead-up to the Full Moon.

The seedling you planted has now sprouted and the roots of your seed have started to form, and they are digging deeper into the soil, gaining strength. Ensure that you are keeping the soil nutritious by giving the plant the water, care, love, and attention that it needs. The roots absorb the nutrients in their environment, giving them to the plant so that it can continue to grow. At this time in the cycle, you need to ask yourself if you are choosing the most nourishing environment for the seed you have planted. If not, perhaps something in your environment needs to be changed.

For example, if your seed of intention was to learn more about Astrology, are you taking the time to research, read books, and talk to others about your experience? Or are you spending time the way you always have? You need to make changes to your environment to make changes to your life. This is what the First Quarter Moon is asking you to do.

This moon phase may also bring up questions about the bigger picture. The small steps you are making now are contributing to a longer-term vision. It's a good time to contemplate what your long-term vision is. Even though this may change, the key aspect of your vision is how you want to feel in the future. Do you want your future self to be filled with joy, gratitude, creativity, or perhaps something else? Now is a good time to remind yourself of your key values, and of the feelings that you want to grow inside of you.

Once you have chosen your key values and feelings, consider how your short-term goals will lead you there. A step-by-step plan will help to keep you on track during this time.

Reflection Question for the First Quarter Moon:

What environment are you creating for your long-term vision to thrive?

Waxing Gibbous (also known as Gibbous Moon)– Feeling Lighter and Brighter

The Waxing Gibbous Moon phase is a time when your fears or worries about your intention will become illuminated. As the light in the sky begins to brighten, you start to uncover some of the aspects of your life that are holding you back from your full potential. These are arising at this moment so that you can prepare to release them or change them under the light of the Full Moon.

All that comes up to the surface is doing so to help you complete this cycle in alignment with your goals. At the same time, as each day becomes brighter, you may start to feel lighter, knowing that the energy of the Moon is supporting you on your journey.

The first shoots of your seed can emerge here. If you have consistently watered your seed, nourished the soil, and taken good care of your intention, the first green shoots will sprout up at this time. The feeling of lightness and brightness allows the shoot to grow past anything that would potentially hold it back. Grow past your old mindset and beliefs, grow past the old version of you. Shed your skin so that the 'new you' can be illuminated and grow toward the Sun.

As you reflect on what is coming up for you at the time of the Waxing Gibbous Moon, it can be helpful to write a list (or create a mental list) of what is holding you back from being the best version of yourself. These limiting beliefs could be showing up around this time as it's just before the Full Moon and everything is being drawn up to the surface.

Some fears that are common at this time could be the fear of not being good enough for the future version of yourself. The fear of not being worthy of receiving the love and success of your future self. Or perhaps the fear of failure. If these fears are coming up, remind yourself that the Moon is supporting you. The energetic forces of stars and sunlight came together to put you on Earth. You are worthy, capable, and fearless enough to live your dreams. More will be revealed, and your fears can be released when the Full Moon shines!

Reflection Question for the Waxing Gibbous Moon:

What fears do you have about your future? What lessons are these fears trying to teach you?

Full Moon – Let Go and Surrender

'Full Moon' means full illumination. Nothing can be kept hidden in the dark, and anything that you thought you tucked away this month to be kept a secret may be rearing its head at this time. This could be the fears you didn't face, the mental or emotional blocks, or the mindset of lack that is holding you back. These aspects of your mind and body are not coming up to worry you; instead, they are coming up because the Moon wants you to let go of them. This is a time to unearth what no longer needs to be hidden inside. To let it all go and surrender.

Your seed of intention has been growing for about two weeks by this stage. Around this time, if the seed is nourished, it will blossom into a beautiful flower. The quality of the flower will reflect how much time and energy you have spent on the foundational aspects of this plant. Are your leaves and petals healthy? What color is your flower blooming in? Is your plant durable enough to withstand the winds and weather conditions? This is the fullest and most healthy expression of your seed (your dream) and you will be able to see it clearly at this time. The Full Moon is a time to see past what has been holding you back and to celebrate the full expression of who you are.

During the Full Moon, imagine the light shining away all darkness, letting go of negativity, limitations, or fears. The Moon is here to support you, so shake it off, write it and burn it, and move your body so that you release the old energy from your cells and create space for the new.

You have set the foundations and done the work, now let go and see what insights you can gain at this time of full illumination. When you can let go, you can see more clearly the insights that are making their way into your life. These ideas and thoughts that arrive at this time are here to help you on the next phases of your journey.

You will find two more chapters about the Full Moon and rituals to use at this time later in the book (Chapters Five and Six).

Reflection Question for the Full Moon:

What are some self-care practices that I can do to release old energy and make space for the new?

Waning Gibbous (also known as Disseminating Moon) – Shedding Layers

The Waning Gibbous Moon comes in the aftermath of 'release'. It is a time to practice gently letting go of the last few things or feelings that are still lingering in your mind and body. Depending on the zodiac sign that ruled the Full Moon, it may have felt emotional, chaotic, uplifting, energetic, or a combination of all the above. Come back to yourself during this time by being gentle with yourself as the last of the old layers shed.

This time is when the old petals of your flower wilt and fall away. It's a time when the dead leaves are shed from the stalk of your plant. As the old peels away, it's a sign of saving energy for the most important parts of your seed. The old energy must be released so that the nutrients can flow into the new aspects of the plant. During this time, notice what naturally falls away. It doesn't have to be a huge upheaval at the roots; instead, it may be more simply the act of release, like a feather falling gently to the earth. As this unfolds, remember that with all death comes rebirth.

Whatever emotions came up for you are now gently subsiding during the Waning Gibbous Moon. It's time to return to a state of balance. Cleansed of the old, ready for the new. During this time, try to stay focused on the final stretch of the cycle. Reset your vision and make your goals realistic. If you continue at a sustainable pace, you could be surprised at how your new reality unfolds.

The work you do during this time should be restorative, to contribute to the foundational aspects of the seed you planted during the New Moon time.

Reflection Question for the Waning Gibbous Moon:

What layers are you shedding right now?

Third Quarter Moon (also known as Last Quarter Moon) – Check-in with Yourself

The Third Quarter Moon means that you are three-quarters through your Moon cycle journey. Just like the first quarter, this is a great time to have another check-in with yourself. Are you ready to step into the final phase?

Spend some time here reflecting on the seed of intention that you planted at the beginning of the cycle (the New Moon). What parts of this intention have already come to fruition? What parts will you focus on in the coming days? What aspects of your environment do you need to shift to continue to nurture your plant in the most nourishing environment?

In terms of the seed, your plant is in a solid state now. It grows freely by itself, moving with its own momentum and assisted by the natural forces that surround it. If the foundations are strong, it shouldn't take too much effort to keep this plant alive. You may even find that as a result of your work, new flower buds pop up, ready to bloom. This is a time when the plant is well-established, sturdy in its roots reaching into the ground, and strong enough to grow tall and reach for the sunlight. There is balance and stability that will be reflected in your emotional state too.

As with all check-ins, be realistic and if you find yourself overwhelmed at this time, you can always save some of your smaller goals for the next cycle. Spend your energy as you feel right but save some for yourself too.

Reflection Question for the Third Quarter Moon:

Is your energy in balance and focused in the right place? Or do you need to make some shifts?

Waning Crescent Moon (also known as Balsamic Moon) – Clear the Slate Before the New Cycle Begins

Although you are working on your dreams, make sure you also have time to slow down around the time of the waning crescent. The light is becoming dimmer, encouraging you to move back inside your body. It may almost feel as though you want to shed the outer layer, to release your physical body and what you no longer need so that you can go inward and evaluate the lessons of this current cycle.

What lessons have you learned since the New Moon? What recurring patterns seem to keep showing up? What does your intuition whisper to you?

During this time, the initial blooming flower, (the fruition of your intention) dies, but its stalk remains standing tall. There are new buds growing on the same plant, sustained by the nourishment of its environment. But if you look closely into the head of the flower that has died, you will find seeds at its core. Shake the old flower and watch as the seeds fall down into the earth, to be planted in the soil. These are your new intentions for the next cycle. Once again, the natural cycle of rebirth begins. A New Moon is on the horizon.

Try to become quiet, gentle, and soft with your words and actions toward yourself during this time. Make space to prepare for the new cycle that's about to begin.

Reflection Question for the Waning Crescent Moon:

What lessons did you learn during the past cycle that you are bringing forward with you into the new cycle?

And the Cycle Continues...

Again and again, through the ages and into the future, the Moon will continue its cyclical path, moving us through these motions each month. Just like the seed and the flower, nature has its rhythms, reflected in all of life here on Earth. These circular patterns keep us in check with ourselves. There are moments of softness and slowness (the yin energy) and there are moments of excitement and extroversion (the yang energy). When these two energies – the yin and the yang – are in balance, all of life flows freely. This state of balance keeps us in a healthy state of equilibrium, the place where dreams, visions, and intentions can bloom.

By following the phases of the Moon and spending time reflecting on the lunar energy as it changes throughout its cycle, you will find that the Moon is a powerful tool for self-development. It provides a space for constant reflection and revaluation which can indicate whether or not you are aligned with your ideal life path and goals.

In this way, the Moon can be the constant marker in your life that helps you to set goals, and to make a plan to achieve these goals. Inviting you to plant a seed each cycle encourages you to take that time to move through life with intention.

Chapter 3

Bonus Material: The Moon & The Zodiac

The Moon and the Zodiac

In a normal calendar year, there are usually twelve New Moons and twelve Full Moons (the only exception to this is when there are thirteen moons – *more on that in the final Chapter*!). In the zodiac, there are also twelve unique signs, which are stellar constellations present in the sky. As the Moon moves through the sky, it also moves through these star constellations. This means that every new month brings a New Moon in a new sign, and consequently, a Full Moon in a new sign too.

The moon moves into a new zodiac sign every two to three days, which means that it will travel through each sign every month, sometimes even visiting a sign twice.

If you have read my first book in this series – Astrology for Beginners – you will remember that each zodiac sign comes with a different energy. Here is a recap of the energies they hold:

Aries – Fiery and action-orientated

Taurus – Grounded and stable

Gemini – Expressive and curious

Cancer – Introverted and emotional

Leo – Bold and outgoing

Virgo – Practical and patient

Libra – Balance and justice

Scorpio – Mysterious and truth-seeking

Sagittarius – Adventurous and unafraid

Capricorn – Resilient and determined

Aquarius – Innovative and individualistic

Pisces – Intuitive and sensitive

Although this is just a brief description of the signs (which are deep and complex in nature), it is enough to predict the type of energy you will experience when the Full or New Moon falls into one of these signs.

For example, during an Aries Full Moon, you can expect a lot of people to be out and about, more expressive and louder than usual. Whereas on a Capricorn Full Moon, you may see people with their heads down working on their goals and dreams with a newfound sense of determination.

As each Moon will provide a different energy, you are given the opportunity to work through different emotional aspects of each cycle. In the following chapters, there are rituals for each Moon sign so that you can understand the energy even better.

Following these rituals, and planting new seeds each month will lead to a blooming garden, full of ripe fruits and beautiful flowers. This will support you to create an abundance of joy as you forge the path into your dream future.

How to Calculate which Sign the Moon is in:

The zodiac signs each rule over a certain time period. A New Moon will always be in the same sign as the current ruling sign, whereas the Full Moon will be in the opposite sign.

The zodiac signs and their dates:

Aries: March 21 - April 19

Taurus: April 20 - May 20

Gemini: May 21 - June 20

Cancer: June 21 - July 22

Leo: July 23 - August 22

Virgo: August 23 - September 22

Libra: September 23 - October 22

Scorpio: October 23 - November 21

Sagittarius: November 22 - December 21

Capricorn: December 22 - January 19

Aquarius: January 20 – February 18

Pisces: February 19 – March 20

So, when a New Moon falls on the dates above, it will correspond directly with that sign.

For example, a New Moon on January 13 will be ruled by Capricorn (*as Capricorn rules the time from December 22 - January 19).*

If a Full Moon falls on the dates above, it will correspond with the opposite zodiac of that sign. The opposite signs are located directly opposite each other in the zodiac wheel.

The opposite signs as pairs are:

Aries + Libra

Taurus + Scorpio

Gemini + Sagittarius

Cancer + Capricorn

Leo + Aquarius

Virgo + Pisces

For example, a Full Moon on October 25 is a Taurus Full Moon. This is because Scorpio rules between October 23 to November 21, but the Full Moon will be ruled by Scorpio's opposite sign: Taurus!

The energy of the zodiac signs will determine the characteristics of each New and Full Moon. As you move into the next chapters, this will become clearer as you start to apply these energies to your Moon rituals and deepen your understanding of the phases of the Moon.

CHAPTER 4

NEW MOON, NEW BEGINNINGS

The New Moon is a time of new beginnings and fresh starts. Here we will dive into the themes that arise around a Full Moon more deeply. This will help you understand all the energetic components of this time in the cycle and what to do (and what not to do) during a New Moon phase.

The Energy of the New Moon

The New Moon is connected with yin energy. This means it is introverted and introspective, and invites you to contemplate your intentions for the next lunar cycle. As we explored previously, each new lunar cycle is a time of new beginnings, a powerful time to plant a seed of intention. That is why yin energy is an important support at this time in the lunar cycle so that you can tune in and listen to your heart's deepest desires.

Although the energy is introverted and introspective, this doesn't necessarily mean that it is a gentle time. Sometimes new insights can really stir up your inner world, pushing you in new directions that you never expected. That's why it is an important time to be gentle with yourself. Diving deep into your mind, body, and emotions can bring up past memories, both joyful and painful. As these memories or new ideas arise, the New Moon presents a wonderful opportunity to sit with these emotions and let them guide you toward your next steps. What you are feeling around a New Moon can help you to formulate a focus for this time period.

The more time you allow for introspection, the louder the voice of your intuition will become. Due to the darkness around the New Moon time, the veils are thin between the conscious and the subconscious. This will give you an opportunity to hear your inner voice more clearly.

For some, their inner voice (sometimes known as intuition) comes as thoughts, words, images, visions, or emotions. You may feel called to listen more deeply to the signs and symptoms that your body is creating if that is how your intuition talks to you. For example, if you have physical pain, your body may be intuitively telling you to rest. If you keep dreaming up certain colors, images, or situations, your mind may be subconsciously guiding you in a certain direction. Perhaps you keep feeling a certain way when you think about a specific dream; this could be your intuition telling you to pursue it!

If you are unsure about your intuition, use the New Moon time to sit with yourself. When you are quiet, and closely listening to your own inner voice, you may hear or see the guidance of your intuition; its message may even surprise you!

You can use tools such as meditation or journaling to try to connect with your inner voice. These tools allow a quietening down of the mental mind so that you can listen to the voice of your own inner healer and wisdom keeper. Once you have connected with your intuition, it is a connection that cannot be severed. That power is with you for life! Perhaps, connecting with your intuition could be your intention for the next New Moon!

What Should I Do on the New Moon?

Around two days before the New Moon, you may start to feel a pull to go inward. A sensation as though you are retracting your energy from the external environment and focusing it on your inner world instead. If you do feel this, listen to the pull. Go within and allow yourself some time to simply be by yourself. In a world that constantly demands our attention and energy, the most nourishing act of self-care can be to spend time alone. Disregard the latest news, the attention-grabbing advertisements, and the loud notifications on your smartphone. Turn it all off, quieten your space, and go inward. There is wisdom waiting for you there!

During the time of the New Moon, there are a few practices you can use to harness the potential of this yin energy. These practices will benefit from the energy that the New Moon is providing on all of Earth at this time. The New Moon energy is strongest at the exact time of the New Moon, but you can tap into its energy two days either before or after this exact time, harnessing the power that the New Moon provides.

At the time of the New Moon, it is beneficial to:

- *Start new projects*
  Using the energy of fresh beginnings will ensure that you start new projects with an eye for detail. This will encourage thorough preparation before launching a new project, and it also allows you the time and space to pick through the content with a fine-tooth comb to straighten out any knots or complications that could arise. Beginning inwards will also set you up for the most beneficial conditions of the project into the long term, which leads us nicely to the next point...

- *Create or launch a new business venture*

  Due to having heightened intuition at the time of the New Moon, you will have a strong sense of what is right or wrong when it comes to creating or launching a business. During the Full Moon, you will be planting the seed of your business into the earth and watching it blossom over the weeks, months, and years to come. Just like any other dream or project that you would set the foundations of during the New Moon time, a new business will also benefit from this foundational energy that is so abundant at this time.

- *Start a new hobby*

  It's a perfect time to try something new. With the energy of growth and potential backing you up, you will be open-minded to new hobbies at this time. It is also a good idea to set a goal for your hobbies when you begin so that you can remember why you started and use that motivation to keep you on track for the long run. For example, start knitting with the goal of finishing a winter sweater, or start painting with the dream of filling a full-sized canvas! This will keep your eyes on the goal, and you'll be inspired as the Moon moves through all of its phases.

- *Create a routine/rituals*

  Starting a new routine, habit, or ritual that you want to be long-lasting is best done at the beginning of a cycle. It doesn't necessarily have to be a Monday, as we've all tried starting a new healthy habit on a Monday morning, and we all know that doesn't work... but starting during a New Moon has more inspiring energy than any old Monday, therefore helping your routine to last longer. It is the foundational time for sowing the seeds that you want to grow over the next few weeks, months, and years. Your new routines will create your new future, so choose them wisely!

- *Make a vision board*

  When you are in a receptive state it is easier to imagine what your future may hold. Listen to your intuitive call here by using pictures, colors, and words as your inspiration. On the next New Moon, try creating a vision board. Grab a few old magazines, cut out the images that inspire you, and glue them onto a big sheet of cardboard to create a visual representation of your dream future! You can spend a few hours lost in your dreams and your creative mind. The vision board does not need to feel 'logical' and it doesn't need to make sense to anybody other than you. Now is simply the time for dreaming up whatever magic you want to manifest in your life. You can do this either by yourself or share the activity with a group of friends (and check in on your dreams regularly to make sure you are all on track!).

- *Think about the future*

  This may seem similar to the last point, but a vision board puts your mind in a dream state, whereas actively thinking about your future can bring you back into the mental world of logic. Spend a little time during the New Moon actively thinking about how you want to achieve your dreams and goals. New Moon time is a great time for planning. Think realistically about where you want to go and how you want to get there. What resources do you need? Who do you need to ask for help? What skills will help you to create this? This leads us nicely to the next point...

- *Make a list*

  A list is a concrete way to get all of your thoughts onto paper. It also gives you a reference to look back at and to remind yourself of those tasks that you wanted to complete. On the New Moon, you could write a list of all the things you want to do during this lunar cycle, the people you want to contact or connect with, the places you want to travel, or even the cafes or restaurants you want to try. Once complete, place this list somewhere visible so that you can check in with your list regularly as the Moon cycle unfolds.

- *Go on a first date or meet new people*

  New Moons also mean new connections. It is a wonderful time for having deep conversations and really getting to know people. As the pace of the world moves slower at this time, your conversations may feel more intimate or more aligned. If you meet under the New Moon, your connections will be meaningful. This makes it a wonderful time to organize a first date or to hang out with a new group of people. It is also a great time for saying yes to new things, which leads us to unexpected invitations...

- *Be open to unexpected invitations – and accept them!*

  Unexpected invitations may pop up during the New Moon time as new plans can emerge spontaneously. Maybe you were asking the Universe for a sign, and this is it! You may have manifested a certain event, connection, or situation where you will find new inspiration. It could be an invitation from someone who can help you bring your business venture, project, or ideas to life. If you are lucky enough to get an unexpected invitation that excites you – it's wise to say yes! The New Moon intuitively aligns people, so that everyone can get the best outcome from the encounter.

- *Create a sacred space*

  Finding or creating a sacred space for yourself during the New Moon will provide a safe place for you to go deep, listen to your intuition, and rest within your yin energy. This place should be for you, for a personal ceremony, or shared only with those you trust. To create a sacred space, you may like to:
  - Find a safe and comfortable place to sit or rest (at home or in nature)
  - Play your favorite music
  - Light a candle
  - Close your eyes and connect with the energy of the New Moon
  - Listen deeply to what your heart says at this time

- *Participate in a ritual*

  A ritual is a specific activity designed to shift the energy in your mind or body, to heighten your intuition, cleanse away the old, or simply inspire you. This can look different for everyone. There are a number of rituals that you can take part in during the New Moon. Check out the next chapter to find twelve rituals for each of the twelve zodiac signs!

What Should I Avoid During the New Moon?

Although all activities are possible under the New Moon, some may not have the best outcome during the time of introspective energy. Although it is not advised to do the following activities, if it is necessary, you can still take part in them. In this case, perhaps they are guiding you to a place of intuition through an unexpected path.

On the day or evening of the New Moon try not to:

- *Take part in high-energy activities*
  Activities that take a lot of energy to execute are considered to be 'yang' activities. These are better saved for the Full Moon when you are ready to express yourself. New Moon time may have you feeling like you want to hide away from the world instead of being out and about in the spotlight. Know that you can always turn down an invitation or say no if your energy is not up for it!

- *Be extra social*
  It's better to let connections flow naturally during New Moon time. Don't push yourself to go out if you really feel like staying in. You'll just regret it and feel more exhausted afterward. Instead, choose to be kind to yourself and listen to what your body wants. Natural connections will arise at this time, which will be aligned with the intentions that you are setting for yourself.

- *Push yourself to your limits*
  One part of knowing your intuition is knowing the limits of your mind and body. Don't exert yourself too much during a New Moon. This is a time to slow down, rest, and recuperate. When the light returns and grows brighter in the sky, that's when you can move into the challenges that face you, but in the

essence of the New Moon, let yourself be still. Rest and recharge to prepare for what the next part of the lunar cycle has in store for you!

Other Cultures and the New Moon

Western cultures are sometimes disconnected from the Moon cycles, with most people not usually participating in any rituals or regular gatherings (except for those who actively follow the Moon phases!). But in the East, many Asian cultures celebrate the New Moon by eating rice cakes, sweets, or fruits to celebrate the sweetness of new beginnings. Every culture celebrates the New Moon a little differently, so let's take a look at some of the most well-known New Moon celebrations.

Countries such as China, South Korea, Vietnam, and Taiwan follow a lunar calendar and celebrate the beginning of their new year on the first New Moon of the lunar calendar. This is the New Moon that falls around January or February. Their celebration date changes yearly depending on the activity in the sky!

In Indian culture, it is believed that the ancestors visit on the evening of the New Moon and therefore a feast should be prepared for these visitors. The veil between those on Earth and those in the spirit world is said to be thin at this time, allowing easy access for the spirits to come and visit their loved ones.

In South Africa, people say that the New Moon is the perfect time to hold a cleansing ceremony. In this culture, they appreciate the cleansing properties of water during this time.

There are many other people around the world celebrating the New Moon in unique ways. Those who follow witchcraft will often head to the woods and commune with the energy of the natural world. Some people in cities will gather in circles to sing and dance and share their intentions for the cycle ahead.

There are many rituals and ways to call in the New Moon energy and in the next chapter we will explore some rituals that you can try too!

Chapter 5

New Moon Rituals & The Zodiac

A ritual is a set of actions used in a ceremonial way to acknowledge something sacred. Rituals have been used for thousands of years, across many cultures to show their gratitude, appreciation, and connection with the world around them. When you connect with a ritual on a regular basis, you are anchoring this practice into your life. You are calling in new energy and new perceptions. Rituals invite you to see the world from a deeper perspective and to acknowledge the unbreakable connection between yourself and the Moon.

How to Prepare for a Ritual:

- *Create time and space for yourself*
  It is important to create a safe space for yourself when you participate in your ritual. To do this, turn off your phone or any distracting devices, if you are living in a shared space, ask those at home to respect your wishes for a few moments of quiet time, and make sure you don't have to rush off anywhere straight afterward. This will limit any distractions and allow you to fully immerse yourself in the activity at hand.

- *Decide if you will do the ritual alone or with friends*
  Both are powerful options. If you choose to do the ritual alone,

this can be a sacred act of self-care and a time to fully express yourself.

If you choose to invite friends, it can be beneficial to speak your intentions out loud and be witnessed by the power of a group. Friends will also keep you accountable with the intentions you set during the New Moon and it can be fun to check in with each other as the cycle progresses.

- *Find your Ritual Tools*
  To enhance the power of the New Moon, it can be nice to create an altar. An altar is a set place in your home where you place a few items such as crystals, things from nature, smudge sticks, photos, your journal, or special objects. These things placed on your altar during the New Moon will remind you of the ceremony and the intentions that you set throughout the rest of the month. You can add or take away items each month, changing the energy to suit the New Moon cycle – for example, bright flowers in Summer, and beautiful leaves in Autumn.

What Sign is the New Moon in?

In this chapter, you will explore a ritual for the New Moon in each of the zodiac signs. You can check the date below to find out what ritual is relevant to the current Moon. Simply take today's date and see what sign it falls under:

Aries: March 21 - April 19

Taurus: April 20 - May 20

Gemini: May 21 - June 20

Cancer: June 21 - July 22

Leo: July 23 - August 22

Virgo: August 23 - September 22

Libra: September 23 - October 22

Scorpio: October 23 - November 21

Sagittarius: November 22 - December 21

Capricorn: December 22 - January 19

Aquarius: January 20 – February 18

Pisces: February 19 – March 20

Note: If the Moon is on the cusp (the first or last day) of a sign, you may need to double-check the Moon phase online to find out exactly what time it will transition into the specific zodiac sign.

A Ritual for Each Moon Sign of the Zodiac

Are you ready for a ritual? Let's begin!

Aries – Light the Spark Within

Aries is a fire sign with bold energy. The New Moon in Aries invites you to acknowledge the flame of your desires and to see what wishes are flickering inside of you, waiting to be cultivated. Aries is unafraid of charging forward and loves embracing new beginnings. In fact, the fire element within Aries encourages the burning away of other people's (or society's) opinions and learning to trust and follow the voice of your own true self.

For this ritual, you will need:

- A candle (and matches)
- Your journal/piece of paper
- Pen to write
- Red clothes or accessories

Start by adorning yourself with your chosen red clothes or bright flashes of red accessories such as a scarf or red jewelry. The color red is sensual, outgoing, and bold, just like Aries. Notice how it feels when you wear this color. Does it make you stand out? Do you feeler brave? Or do you feel uncomfortable? Simply notice how the color red makes you feel. Red holds a passionate energy, and this will help you to connect with your own inner passion. The more connected to your passions, the more comfortable you may feel and vice versa – if you are disconnected from your passions, red might feel awkward and uncomfortable for you.

Take a seat with your candle and matches. Before lighting the candle, take the candle in your hands and hold it in line with your heart space. Take a few moments to think about what is residing in your heart right now. What dreams and wishes are dancing in the fire of your heart, waiting to be fulfilled?

Now it's time to illuminate these dreams. Light your candle and place it down in front of you. Watch the flame as it dances in the surrounding air. See how it flickers and moves. For the next five to ten minutes, sit quietly with your candle. You may like to imagine that this candle also resides within your heart. This flame is alive within you too. It is the flame of your biggest wish, and the light shines upon any secret dream or hidden desire you have in your heart.

When you are ready, turn to your journal or paper and answer the following questions:

1. What has your inner flame illuminated?
2. What message does your heart want you to hear?
3. The heart invites you to follow it and to listen to its wishes. How will you do this?

By writing down these answers, you have a reminder of your New Moon intention. Maybe you want to add these answers to your altar for the month or keep them somewhere sacred.

If no direct messages are coming up, sit with it a bit longer. You will need to move your mind aside to let the heart speak.

You can also ask for other signs or confirmations of what you heard over the coming days. Be open to receiving this guidance!

Taurus – Power of Planting

Taurus is an earth sign, grounded in nature and fond of earthly pleasures and comfort. Taurus has a long-term focus and is always in things for the long run. This is a beneficial quality when looking at building something for the future. Doing the groundwork now will set you up to reach your goals at a steady and progressive pace.

For this ritual, you will need:

- A seed of a plant or flower - something you want to grow

- A beautiful plant that needs potting; one that brings you joy!
- Enough soil to fill your chosen pot
- A cup of water
- A dream or wish
- Biodegradable paper (optional if not available)

Prepare your materials before the New Moon so that you are ready for your ritual. On the day or evening of the New Moon, gather all of the items and recall your dream or wish.

The wish that you choose will be infused into the essence of the plant. The plant will reflect your wish, growing either fast or slow, healthy, or unhealthy, depending on your commitment to your own wish. So, be sure to think carefully about the intention that you will grow.

Once you have your wish (or dream) clear in your mind, write it down in simple words on biodegradable paper. *If you don't have biodegradable paper, you can write it on normal paper.*

Next, fill your pot with soil, knowing that this is the foundational element for your dreams to come to fruition. As you put the soil in the pot, think about what foundations you need to have in your life to build your dream. Jot these down in your journal if you like. Take the paper that you wrote your wish on and plant that piece of paper in the soil now. It will go underneath the seed.

When the soil is in the pot, the seed is ready to be planted. Hold the seed in your hand and whisper a little wish to it. Set your intention clearly, knowing that this seed will grow in the way that you wish. It will reflect your intentions. When you are ready, place the seed into the soil, pushing it down into the darkness.

Take your cup of water and feel the weight of the water in your hands. The water is the positive action that you will take to work toward your dream or wish. Simply setting an intention won't grow the plant, but taking positive action will!

Pour your water over the seed, reminding you of the steps you need to take next to bring your plant to life.

Each day, spend some time with your plant (and your dream!), watering it, reaffirming your actions, and watching it grow. Good things take time to grow, but the journey will be worth it!

Gemini – Musical New Moon

Gemini is an air sign, one that is social, chatty, and intelligent. Ruled by the mind, Gemini is often stuck in thoughts, formulating opinions, or coming up with new ideas. The energy is both curious about life and progressive in its visions. With a playful New Moon comes a playful ritual.

For this ritual, you will need:

- A music platform with a shuffle function (wherever you normally find your music)
- An open and curious mind

Music is connected with the energy of air, traveling across space and putting a feeling or emotion into our minds and bodies.

To begin this ritual, take a moment to ask the musical Universe what you need to receive this Moon cycle. If you have a certain question and you are looking for answers, you can connect with this question.

Alternatively, if you don't have a specific question right now, you can ask for words of wisdom, inspiration, or guidance that will be helpful to hear.

Take three deep breaths to connect with your question or intention.

Take your music, and if you have a large playlist you can use it, or otherwise tap into the larger music library, and then hit shuffle. This will ensure that your choice of song is completely random.

Listen to the words (or if instrumental, the sounds) that play. The music gods and goddesses have provided you with some insight. This song has a message for you in it. Can you hear what that message is?

You might need to write down some of the lyrics if you need more clarity. When you find the part that resonates with you, you will know it!

Take a few moments to consider what this message means for you on the New Moon. How will you use this message to move forward with your new beginnings?

Use this ritual anytime you want to receive a musical message.

Cancer – Cozy Like a Crab

Cancer is a water sign, deeply emotional and connected to its feelings. The Cancer New Moon is a deep time of introspection, of going inwards into your shell and making yourself feel comfortable. From a place of comfort, you can build foundational spaces around you that encourage growth and expression of your truest self.

For this ritual, you will need:

- A homely space
- A few items that are special to you
- A warm blanket

Find a really comfortable and cozy nook in your home. This place should feel safe to you, allowing you to completely relax and surrender, quietening your mind and releasing any tension from the body.

This ritual is about creating a shell around you and feeling cozy like a crab. First, lay out your chosen blanket on the floor. It doesn't matter how big or small it is. Notice the texture of it, and how it makes you feel. What else does this blanket remind you of?

Now, wander around the space you are in and gather a few items that are special to you. These could be gifts, photographs, or things that remind you of special people or special times in your life. When you have a few things in your hands, take them over to your cozy nook.

Take a few of your special items and place them on the blanket. Perhaps you are sitting in the middle of the blanket and place these items around you, or maybe you are to the side of the blanket, and you let these items cover the blanket fully. Place them down with care and love, knowing that they are special items to you.

How does it feel to have these special items in the space of your blanket? What does it feel like to be surrounded by and reminded of all the things that you hold dearly in your heart? What does each item mean to you?

Is there anything missing from your blanket? Can you write about it or find a photo of it and add it to your special space now too?

During this New Moon, be gentle with yourself and simply take some time to rest on your blanket with your special items. Reflect on how wonderful it is to have collected all of these memories and connected with special people. How does it feel to be surrounded by all this love?

Bathe in the special environment for as long as you enjoy! You may even like to keep the blanket and items out for a few days, as a place to return to when you need comfort or support.

Leo – Express Yourself!

Leo is bold, bright, and brilliant. The fire energy of Leo invites you to be unapologetically you. It's a time of opening your heart to new possibilities and learning how to dedicate your time and energy toward yourself.

For this ritual, you will need:

- An expressive outfit
- Bold accessories
- Courage

Gather up your inner courage and step into this challenge today. Sometimes the biggest challenge we can face in life is being our true selves.

Today on this New Moon, make a commitment to yourself that you will be who you want to be. Listen to the wishes of your inner voice. What does the truest version of you look like?

Head over to your wardrobe (or if you feel that your wardrobe no longer represents who you are, you can go to a second-hand clothing store!)

Take a look around at what catches your attention. Are there any items of clothing that you have but have been too afraid to wear? Are there any accessories that have been waiting for you to wear them? Think about that bold sweater, the dress that makes a statement, or the extra high heels.

As you pick items to wear today, think about how your outfit can express how you are feeling on the inside. Try something new, choose something that you wouldn't normally wear.

Maybe it's a few accessories that make you stand out; a red feather in your hair, a crown of flowers, bright makeup, or diamond-studded shoes. There must be something in your wardrobe that you wish to put on but think it's a little 'too much'. Well today, it's not – there is no such thing as 'too much' under a Leo sign.

Now once you've dressed up, gather your courage and head out for a stroll. Walk with your shoulders back and heart open. If you weren't planning on going anywhere today then head out for a cup of coffee in your authentic outfit or visit a friend.

This is the beginning of the new you.

Virgo – Bare Foot Connection

Virgo is an earth sign, one who likes practicality, patterns, and plans. Under the Virgo New Moon, there may be an extra sense of needing to have everything together, or a need to know what your purpose is and where your life is headed. This can be a great time for planning and preparing for the future, but, in a stressful state this planning is done from the head and not the body. To shake up this rigid energy and reconnect with your natural energy, here is a ritual.

For this ritual, you will need:

- A place in nature (or a patch of grass/sand/stone)
- Bare feet

Head out to a place in nature. This could be a local park, the ocean side, or the mountains. If you don't have much nature available to you at this time, try to find a small patch of grass or a garden.

Take off your shoes and place your bare feet on the earth. Feel the textures of the earth, the temperature either warm or cool. Feel the elements, and notice if the earth is damp or dry. What do you feel beneath your feet? Stand still and simply breathe, deep belly breaths in and out of your body, connecting with the earth below.

Think about where you want to go in the next few weeks or months. What does your life journey have in store for you? Without getting too caught up in the details, can you think about the next few steps you need to take?

For example, if you want to move to start a new hobby, maybe your steps look like this:

Step one: Search for a local group that participates in this hobby.

Step two: Book the first class.

Step three: Show up to the class and learn your chosen new skill.

Step four: Repeat the hobby and participate on a regular basis.

Now, with your feet back on the earth, you will formulate your own steps in terms of the direction you wish to walk in.

When you are ready, take the first step and feel how it lands on the earth. Root it down, ground into it, and connect it with your first step of action. Then take the next step, connecting your physical step with your second step of action. Continue in this way and see where the journey takes you. Allow the steps to guide you as you discover the action to take after this New Moon.

You might find that you are walking super slow as you connect each step with your next right action – and that's great! This walking meditation is meant to connect you more deeply with each intention, as you really embody each step.

When your journey feels complete, come back to stillness. Take a few deep breaths with both feet planted on the ground and know that you have rooted your intention firmly into the earth. And so the real action begins....

Libra – Returning to Balance

Libra is about balance and is constantly working to return to a place of equilibrium. Libra values trust, harmony, and love, working to find a way that all three of these values can co-exist in their life. Ruled by air, there is a strong mental element in the mind of Libras. This ritual will work with the mental energy to clear the old and make space for the new.

For this ritual, you will need:

- Two pieces of paper
- A pen
- Time to think

Take one piece of paper, and at the top of your page write the words:

"What do I THINK would be good for me?"

On the second piece of paper, write the words:

"What do I ALREADY DO that makes me feel good?"

Beneath each heading, write a list of the things you do that make you feel healthy, nourished, and whole, and then write a list of the things you think would help you, or perhaps you 'wish' you were doing them. Although the questions may sound similar, this is a ritual to acknowledge the beneficial practices in your life, and to appreciate them! At the same time, it invites you to think of other practices that could be helpful for you that you haven't yet tried.

As Libra is about balance, this New Moon is a time to find balance between the old and the new. What old habits can you replace with new ones, so that all areas of your life start to feel good?

Include things like your lifestyle, food choices, exercise, friends you hang out with, hobbies you want to try, etc. Try to think outside the box!

On this New Moon, circle one practice from each list and give it a go in the next day or two! Feel the difference between returning to an old self-care practice, and challenging yourself to try a new one!

Maybe, you would even like to extend the challenge to try three things on the new list during this Moon cycle! Now that you've got the list of inspirations, let it guide you toward creating the future you!

Scorpio – The Mystical Moon

The water sign Scorpio lives in the underworld, unafraid of the spiritual realms, in touch with its intuition, and deeply connected to the rhythms of nature. Mystery is available and accessible to everyone if you allow yourself to drop deep enough. Under the dark Moon, the energy is perfect for dropping into your spiritual side.

For this ritual, you will need:

- A crystal chosen intuitively by yourself (if a crystal is not available to you, take a stone from nature)
- A comfortable place to sit (with a cushion or chair if necessary)
- A warm blanket to make yourself extra comfortable
- Journal and pen

This is a time to go deep into the mystic and spiritual side of you.

Gather your crystal (or stone) and set yourself up in a comfortable place where you can sit easily. Connect your hips firmly into the earth beneath you and raise your spine tall, growing the crown of your head toward the sky.

Take hold of the crystal in your hands, closing your hands around it. Your crystal will act as the anchor to drop you deeper into your body.

Close your eyes and connect with your breath.

Imagine that you have placed your crystal in a deep blue ocean. As you drop it into the water, your crystal begins to sink to the bottom of the ocean.

Holding on, you drop with your crystal moving down, down, down, deeper into the water.

As you move down through the ocean, imagine that you are dropping deeper down into yourself too. Deeper into your subconscious.

If thoughts arise, or you get distracted, then simply bring your attention back to the breath, back to the image of the ocean.

Drop deeper with each breath until you touch all the way down to the sea floor. Once you have touched down on the sand or rock below, find stillness. Stillness in your mind and your body.

What do you see or perceive to be around you?

How do you feel down here in these depths?

What is the deeper part of yourself trying to communicate with you?

Once you have your answers, or you have enjoyed the stillness for long enough, slowly return, floating back up to the surface.

Write down the answers that came to you.

Sagittarius – Surprise Adventure!

Sagittarius is a fire sign that likes to connect with free-spirit energy. It has an adventurous outlook on life, unafraid to venture to new places, often with a sense of spontaneity. This ritual will harness the adventurous spirit of Sagittarius to take you on a new adventure.

For this ritual, you will need:

- A map (either online or printed) of your region, state, country, or if you are feeling super adventurous, a map of the world!
- If using a printed map, you'll need a pencil
- A sense of adventure!

Begin by taking a look at your map. The map represents how far you could potentially travel in the next weeks or months, so ensure that it is realistic for your current life situation. For example, if you can travel for a few hours, choose a regional map. If it is possible for you to take a weekend trip interstate, choose a map of your whole country. If it is possible for you to plan a big trip, choose a world map!

Now, take a breath and close your eyes. With your map in front of you, point to a place on the map. If you have an online map, simply point with your finger. If you have a printed map, make a little circle on your map (while keeping your eyes closed).

Once you've chosen a spot – Open your eyes!

Pack your bags – you are going on an adventure. This New Moon time in Sagittarius is a perfect time for dreaming up a holiday and making plans. Choose a day or certain dates that you will take to travel to your chosen location.

Whether you have landed in a major city or a remote small town, there is something there waiting for you! Trust in the magic of New Moons, and let your intuition guide you.

Fulfilling your spirit with a sense of spontaneous adventure is a great way to celebrate new beginnings, find new inspirations, and have a new perspective on life.

Enjoy!

Capricorn – New Inspiration

Capricorn is an earth sign, with an analytical mind. Sometimes getting stuck in old habits, Capricorn may need a bit of a shake-up to create some change. Practical, level-headed, and internally wise, Capricorn takes its time in making decisions, and in doing so, moves with determination, patience, and focus.

Capricorn is the ultimate planner who likes to take life step-by-step.

For this ritual, you will need:

- 1 A4 piece of paper
- A pen
- Time

On the day of the New Moon, take time to think about new things that you have wanted to try, but haven't yet found the time (or are feeling afraid to begin). To move in a methodical way (the way Capricorn likes it), you are going to make a 29-day plan to try something new each day. That's just over 4 weeks of new activities and one whole Moon cycle to really solidify this new and adventurous attitude to life.

Take your piece of paper and write the numbers 1 to 28 in a column. Next to each number, write down one new thing you will try. These can be small or large, for example, order a new drink at your regular café, try a new class, bake a new fancy cake, run a certain distance, or call a friend you have fallen out of touch with.

It would be best to break it up between small and larger tasks so that you have a variety of change in your week, and this will also help to keep it realistic and achievable.

All the way through this Moon cycle and until the next New Moon, try one new thing each day. Cross these off the list after they are completed.

At the end of the cycle, take some time to reflect on what has changed through this ritual:

Has your mind become more flexible, or more creative? Do you feel more confident? Take some notes to remind yourself of how the changes affected you! Is this a trend that you would like to continue?

Aquarius – Wild, Weird, and Wonderful

The ultimate free-thinker and freedom promoter, Aquarius is an air sign that is up in the clouds. Leader of revolutions, with a humanitarian heart, this sign is full of unique ideas of how to change the world and make it a better place for all living beings.

For this ritual, you will need:

- A large piece of paper (A3 size), or a Canvas
- Colored pencils, watercolor paints, or other art paint
- A creative perspective

Under the energy of the Aquarius New Moon, a time for inventing new ideas and sharing them boldly, think of your ideal world. Dream up your best future, considering the following aspects of your dream work.

1. What people are you surrounded by?

2. What place are you living in?

3. What food are you eating?

4. What does your surrounding environment look like?

When you have an image in your mind, take it to the paper! But rather than try to accurately depict the image in your mind, allow your creative mind to run free.

You may like to create an abstract depiction of your dream future, e.g. a stroke of purple represents a connection with your friends. A yellow circle may remind you of your inner power or the golden sun. Let your creation be personal to you.

Once it is complete, stay in your creative mind, your dream state, and reflect back on what you created.

Is this dream far off in the future or do you think you can call it in closer and make it a reality?

On this New Moon, think about the small steps you can take this month, to move closer to your dream world! Aquarian energy believes in you!

Pisces – Cleansing Bath

Pisces, the last sign of the zodiac, is the fish that swims in the watery and emotional depths. New Moons in Pisces can easily evoke tears, and you may experience deeper emotions during this lunar transition. These tears are shed to lighten your body, to release old pain, and to recreate who you are so that you can start fresh. The following ritual will help with this cleansing process.

For this ritual, you will need:

- A body of water (this could be a bath in your home, a lake, the ocean, or a running river)
- Crystals, candles, and items that are sacred to you
- A handful of herbs and flowers, collected from the forest or garden

On the day or evening of the New Moon, you are invited to take a bath, whether that's in the comfort of your own home, or the wild waters of nature!

To prepare for this time of rest and reset of your body, mind, and soul, you want to create a bath with intention. By setting a personal intention for yourself at this time, you will infuse the waters with healing energy.

To begin, take your candle and light it. This brings the energy of light into your surroundings, illuminating old wounds so that they can be released now.

Place your flowers or herbs that you collected into the water. If you are in a bath, they will float there. If you are in nature, notice the way these plants move on the water. This is an offering to Earth, to thank it for holding us in this healing space.

If you have crystals with you, place them in the water. Water cleanses crystals, and the crystals can amplify the intention that you set at the beginning. Let the crystal rest in the water, infusing its energy into your bath.

Now, remembering your intention (whether it's to cleanse, energize, empower, or something else entirely), hold it within your mind as you step into the water. Immerse yourself fully in the healing space that you have created. Breathe deeply and imagine the water moving in and through your body. Here you are cleansing all the old energy, the stress, the fears, the worries, and leaving it behind for the water to hold. When you have had enough time in the water – as little or as much as you'd like – gently make your way out of the bath. Feel the energy in your body and mind, alive, yet soothed, empowered, and optimistic for the New Moon cycle ahead.

The Importance of the Ritual

Taking time for these rituals on the New Moon will set the tone for the entire month ahead. If you use the time wisely to plant your seeds and dreams, you will have a direction to follow and an action plan to inspire you as you stay on track throughout the Moon cycle.

One of the best ways to ensure that you work with these rituals is to mark your calendar at the time of the New Moon, pre-read the applicable ritual within this book, gather up the things you'll need, and then set aside an hour to make it happen. The more often you turn to rituals, the more natural it will become as time goes on.

Before you know it, and with the help of the rituals, you'll be powerfully manifesting with the Moon!

Chapter 6

The Full Moon: A Time to Let Go

The brightest nights are those illuminated by Full Moons. It's the easiest Moon phase to spot in the sky as half of the Moon's surface is fully illuminated and shining toward us on Earth.

You may already be quite familiar with the energy of the Full Moon as you have surely gazed in awe as you watched it move through the night sky. Think about the last time you stood outside staring up at the Full Moon. How did that big bright energy make you feel?

This energy can differ slightly from month to month, depending on what zodiac sign the Moon is moving through, but at the same time, it will have a similar effect on most people (whether they believe it or not!). The more often you tune into the Full Moon energy, the more familiar you will become with its effects. This will help you to harness the power of the Full Moon and to include its energy in your daily practices. By using Full Moon energy you'll find a new depth of expansion as you head toward your greatest potential.

The Energy of the Full Moon

The Full Moon is one of the most energetic times of the month. You may start to notice this energy a few days before the Moon is full as your sleeping patterns can change, and you can feel more energized (or maybe even a little chaotic!). Plans might suddenly change, or unexpected visitors pop by. You may feel that your energy is wired, or that you are floating through the day without really feeling grounded. It may also be a time when a million thoughts are running through your mind at once! Perhaps even raising a feeling of anxiety within you... Although these are the most common feelings that people experience around the Full Moon time, everybody will feel the Moon's energy a little differently. For this reason, it's important to try to become more aware of your body and notice what the Moon is trying to tell you during a Full Moon transition. The Moon likes to communicate through thoughts and feelings that you experience in your body. So listen to those signs and signals that are being sent your way!

Another powerful aspect of the Full Moon is its power to illuminate the truth. The Full Moon shines light on what is hidden inside of you. It is especially good at uncovering those things you thought you had buried deep enough to remove them from your life. These may surface when the Full Moon is in the sky, urging you to unveil them and complete the necessary work to move through them.

If you have had a tough month but neglected to acknowledge it (and perhaps you have been dealing with stress by turning to distractions), you won't be able to push down this stress any longer. Expect it to come out with flying colors. The same goes for you if you had an emotional event happen during the last month and you just pressed it down inside of you. During the Full Moon, you won't be able to ignore it any longer as this is a time when it will rise up to be seen and heard.

This energy of bringing everything to the surface can be overwhelming. It makes the Full Moon time fairly emotional and sometimes very challenging. The truth is, the energy of this time will depend on what you have or have not dealt with over the past cycle. Although this can feel like a punishment, the Full Moon is actually a time for great insights, action, and healing. If you can shine a positive light on a difficult situation, you may find that things start to change for the better.

Anything that arises for you during Full Moon time is usually coming up for one of two reasons:

Number One: This Aspect of Life is Calling for Attention

Think about health issues, friendships, relationships, work commitments, or whatever else surfaces during a Full Moon – the themes that show up dramatically are asking you to look closely at what you are doing to support these themes in your life (or look at what you have neglected to do!).

When things arise under the Full Moon, it means it is time to deal with them in a new way. You may need to be creative and think about solutions you haven't tried before. You may notice that spontaneous ideas or newfound clarity can arrive during this time too. If you choose to address these issues, it will be a healing time for you.b

Number Two: This Aspect of Your Life Wants to be Released

The Full Moon is a powerful time for cleansing and letting go. Any issues that pop up during this time may be saying one last goodbye. Notice what comes up and think about how you can let it go out of your life.

If this is a person, maybe an authentic conversation is needed to re-establish your boundaries. If it's an old item that brings up emotional attachment, it could be time to pass it on to another owner. Whatever it is, think about a way that you can remove it from your life in a healthy and beneficial way. The more you can let go of the old, the lighter you will feel without any old baggage hanging around.

Let Go, Release and Cleanse

It's easy to say let go, release, and cleanse, but what does that actually mean?

Your body is very energetic and receptive to other people's energies, as well as the energy of certain places and things. To maintain a healthy state of being, you also need to maintain healthy energetic boundaries. This means saying yes to things that light you up, and no to things that drag you down.

A time of both release and closure, the Full Moon can be a great time to set boundaries relating to what you do and don't allow into your life. *What people do you need to have a conversation with about how they are impacting your life?* They might show up during this time. *What boundaries do you need to set in your workplace to help you reduce stress?* Perhaps a conversation about this will happen on the Full Moon.

Sometimes you need to instigate these conversations, and the Full Moon's energy will support you. Its bright light will bring clarity to both parties and will help to find a clear solution and path forward. Be brave enough to address these issues when the full moon is in the sky. Just be aware, that emotions may be running high for all parties at this point, but it will help the truth to come out!

The more you can let go of (both physically and energetically), the lighter you become. This creates new space in your body, mind, and energy for what you really want to pursue. It can create space for new ideas to come into your life. As the Full Moon is a wonderful time for dreaming you might notice more intense or visual dreams during your sleep. Emotions are also heightened at this time, which can help you to determine what dreams and ideas you really want to follow.

Full Moon illumination provides a portal for quick changes to occur and big energies to be called in. At this time hold your vision of the future in clear view and keep working toward it. The Moon is supporting your actions!

Altering your Altar

If you created an altar (sacred space) on the New Moon, you may now want to make a few small changes during the Full Moon. Full Moon energy may encourage you to add more inspiration to your altar, adding extra items, poems, photos, or things that light you up!

Alternatively, in terms of letting go, you may want to take away some of the items from your altar, releasing the old energy that is attached to it. For example, if you wrote a letter on the New Moon, you may like to burn it under the Full Moon to release its intention out into the world.

Another wonderful practice to recall the energetic intentions that you set at the beginning of the Moon cycle is to take one of the items from your New Moon altar and carry it with you on the day of the Full Moon. This will amplify the intention of your New Moon wishes and dreams. It will also be a reminder of the goal that you are working towards.

Aside from the altar, there are a few other practices that can be done on the Full Moon and a few that you should try to avoid if possible. Let's explore these.

What to Do on a Full Moon

When the energy is high and the sky is bright, try some of these ideas:

- *Fire Burning Ceremonies*
  If you feel something coming up for release, a wonderful way to let it go is to write it on a piece of paper and burn it with a flame. It could be the flame of a small candle, or it could be a raging bonfire. This practice lets the energy of the old be released to make space for the new.

- *Tune into what you are feeling*
  As mentioned above, emotions can be running high at this time of the Moon cycle. Take a moment to sit or stand under the Full Moon and breathe deeply. Feel what is happening inside of you. Notice what emotions are bubbling under the surface. Allow these emotions to be expressed now rather than bubble away for another few Moon cycles, where they will only grow in intensity. Expressing these emotions could look like; writing about them, screaming outrage or anger, talking to a friend, crying, or dancing them out of the body - which takes us to the next suggestion!

- *Moving the Body*
  Moving the body with high-intensity exercise, ecstatic dancing or shaking helps to get the electrical energy running through your body. It charges up the cells and makes you feel alive. If you can, stand under the Full Moon, play an upbeat song, and just let your body move in whatever way it wants to express itself.

- *Ground the Lunar Energy*

As this time is highly charged with energy, emotions, and maybe even ecstatic dance, it's important to come back to a calm state of being. To do this, it's important to ground the lunar energy down into your body. If you are feeling overwhelmed during a Full Moon, place both of your feet on the earth and breathe deeply. Imagine the moonlight traveling into the crown of your head, down through your spine, and into the earth through the soles of your feet. This way, you are moving the charged energy (anxiety, fear, or overwhelm) out of the mind and down into the earth to help you feel connected, grounded, calm, and centered. It's especially good to do this before driving on the night of the Full Moon!

- *Clearing and Cleansing*
  In alignment with the cleansing energy of the Full Moon, it can be a wonderful time to cleanse your personal energetic field. To do this, you can use a smudge stick or incense and cleanse with smoke. You can also use running water, whether from the shower, river, or ocean, to take the old energy away. Or you can stand in the breeze, with your feet on the earth, feeling the wind whisk away the old, stuck energy you've been carrying.

- *Rituals!*
  Similarly to the previous chapter, the following chapter has 12 unique rituals for you to do with each Full Moon of the zodiac. These will encourage you to move deeper into the energy of each sign ruling the Full Moon.

What to Avoid on the Full Moon

- *Risky activities*

At this time of rush, charged emotions, and unpredictability, it's best to avoid any risky activities under the Full Moon. It can be easy to skip over safety steps at this time, or to miss critical information. If there is no chance to reschedule your activity, make sure you double-check everything before you begin!

- *Travel*
  Although it may seem amazing to travel with the light of the Full Moon guiding your way, it is also a time of more confusion and chaos. For this reason, travel plans may be delayed or rescheduled wreaking havoc on your holiday. For this reason and to avoid disappointment, try not to travel on Full Moon days. Instead, book your plane tickets, trains, and buses for another time.

- *Avoid new beginnings*
  The New Moon is the place for new beginnings, not the Full Moon. With high energy, the Full Moon wants to clear and cleanse anything that's not necessary for your life, so starting a new habit now might mean that it will not last in the long run.

- *Don't rush*
  Try to be extra mindful during Full Moon transits. Take your time, move with mindfulness, and allow extra time for you to arrive early at an event or place so that any unexpected delays or interruptions won't make you feel stressed.

- *Try to reschedule intense meetings or discussions*
  If there is a big topic on the table, or an important discussion that needs to be had, try to save it for a day when the full moon is not ruling! During the full moon, if both parties are

energetically charged, intense meetings or conversations may create more conflict rather than resolution. If it is impossible to reschedule, go into the meeting with the intention to listen and respond rather than to quickly react!

Full Moon Cultural and Traditional Celebrations

The Full Moon has long been worshipped in various cultures for its powerful energy.

In India, people visit sacred rivers and bodies of water to cleanse both their physical and spiritual selves. The Hindu religion celebrates 'Purnima' (the day of the Full Moon) as a time of prosperity and happiness. During this day, they fast from sunrise to sunset and pray to Lord Vishnu. After a day of fasting and praying, they enjoy some light food at dusk and swim in a river (if accessible).

Japan celebrates the Full Moon with night-time Moon-viewing ceremonies known as Tsukimi. This is a time of gathering to celebrate the beauty of the Moon and to enjoy traditional foods together.

In Mexico, some people utilize the indigenous practice of Native Americans and take part in a Moon dance. This is a dance focused on praying and dancing for the sake of healing while worshipping feminine energy and Mother Earth. This ceremonial celebration can take up to three days, during which the nights are for dancing and sharing sacred teachings under the moonlight, and the days are for resting.

The people who follow the path of Paganism (sometimes called witchcraft) use Moon rituals to worship the Moon as a Goddess, especially one connected with fertility. They acknowledge the cycles of life and use many cleansing rituals such as burning sage and singing and dancing in sacred circles.

No matter how you choose to celebrate the New Moon, the most important lesson is to listen to the whispers of the Full Moon as they are told through your own body and emotions. You can explore this through the rituals in the next chapter!

CHAPTER 7

FULL MOON RITUALS & THE ZODIAC

The Full Moon is a potent time for rituals as the energy is more amplified than usual. This charged-up energy illuminates your ideas and dreams, making the Full Moon time perfect for letting go of whatever restrictions are holding you back.

The following rituals are specific for each of the zodiac signs. As each sign holds a unique energy, each ritual is unique to encompass that specific energy.

Before you begin, find out what sign the next Full Moon is in. You can look at the dates listed below:

Libra Full Moon falls between: March 21 – April 19

Scorpio Full Moon falls between: April 20 – May 20

Sagittarius Full Moon falls between: May 21 - June 20

Capricorn Full Moon falls between: June 21 – July 22

Aquarius Full Moon falls between: July 23 – August 22

Pisces Full Moon falls between: August 23 – September 22

Aries Full Moon falls between: September 23 – October 22

Taurus Full Moon falls between: October 23 – November 21

Gemini Full Moon falls between: November 22 – December 21

Cancer Full Moon falls between: December 22 – January 19

Leo Full Moon falls between: January 20 – February 18

Virgo Full Moon falls between: February 19 – March 20

Remember - the Full Moon signs are the opposite of the New Moon signs during the same time period! Also, if the Full Moon falls on the first or last day of the dates above, it's best to look online to check exactly what sign the Moon is in, as it could be on the cusp.

The Rituals

Once you've got the sign you are working with, pre-read your ritual before the Full Moon arrives. This will help you gather your materials and set aside your time for the ritual.

Aries – Fire Ritual

Aries feels comfortable playing with fire. It is a sign that knows how to stoke the coals and turn them back into a flame. It is also a sign that finds it easy to shake off the old, or the negative and let it go. No time for resentment when there is an adventure to be had!

For this ritual, you will need:

- A candle (or if you have access and space for it, you can have a bonfire)
- Paper and pen

- Any old letters or journals you want to burn or release
- A glass or bottle of water

If possible, go for a bonfire or a fire in a fireplace for this Full Moon. The bigger the flames, the better for reminding you of the wildfire nature within you. Of course, if this is not possible (please don't burn down the house!), take a candle and a small burn-proof bowl. Keep a bottle of water nearby to put out any stray flames.

With your pen and paper, you will write down a few things you are ready to let go of.

At the top of your page, write the words:

'Under this Aries full moon, I am releasing...'

Then underneath, write what you are ready to burn. This could be old habits, feelings that have been lingering too long, or even letting go of the need to know or to control a certain outcome.

When you feel that you've written it all down, take a look at your words and really feel them. Read your words out loud, let them be heard and witnessed by the fire.

Take a deep breath, and then place them into the flames (or into the fireproof bowl and light it with the candle if you're indoors).

Watch as the paper transforms, disintegrating, releasing its previous form. Feel yourself become lighter as these words, feelings or situations are released from you.

If there is anything else you need to burn today, such as an old diary or journal, place it in the fire too!

When you feel complete, and the fire has dwindled, pour your bottle or glass of water over the ashes. When cool, take these ashes and return them to the earth. You may place them in your garden, or some other natural environment where Mother Earth will look after them. Nature will take your old energy and transform it into new growth as the cycle continues.

This completes the alchemical process – air, fire, water, and earth – the four major elements coming together to help you release and reset under the power of the Full Moon!

Taurus – Root to Rise

Taurus, the earthly creature, likes to create a steady home base. Most people think this means creating a physical home or house, but actually, when you realise that home is a place within you, you can learn to create safety and comfort within yourself. Taurus helps you to remember this, as it is a sign that likes to take care of the physical body. To find this home within yourself, you can try the following ritual.

For this ritual, you will need:

- Bare feet
- Somewhere to look at the Full Moon
- A patch of earth

Find a spot under the light of the Full Moon. If the weather allows, stand outside with your bare feet planted on the earth. If it's too cold, you may choose to stand by a window where the Full Moon is in view. If you cannot see the Moon, imagine its bright moonlight shining from behind the clouds.

Ground yourself into your standing spot. Do this by moving into the yogic pose '*tad asana*', meaning mountain pose. To get into tad asana:

Plant your feet about hip-width apart. Lift all ten of your toes off the ground, spread them wide and then one by one plant them back onto the ground. Really press your toes into the floor or earth, gripping the base beneath you. From here, take a small, slight bend in the knees and feel the weight of your body drop down into your feet.

Tuck your pelvis under to align the spine and then imagine a string attached to the top of your head, like that of a puppet, pulling you up toward the sky. Relax your shoulders away from your ears. Allow your arms to rest heavily by your side. Activate your hands and spread your fingertips wide, pointed toward the ground.

From this place, feel the strength in your body. Feel the connection between your feet and the earth below. Feel the connection between the top of your head and the sky above. Imagine roots growing from the soles of your feet into the earth below. Also, feel the strings from your head reaching up into the stars and connecting with the light of the Full Moon.

You exist between the earth and the sky (or spirit). You are the physical formation of your own home at this time on Earth. To cleanse your home and your body, you will take a few deep breaths.

As you breathe in, draw your breath up from the earth, through your feet and up your spine, allowing it to fill your entire body. As you breathe out, it moves out through the crown of your head and up into the sky.

On your next inhale, draw your breath in from the light of the Full Moon, draw it in through your head, down your spine and all the way into your arms and legs. On the exhale, breathe it out through your feet and back into the earth.

Repeat this pattern for three to five minutes, or longer if it feels good.

Inhale the earth's energy up into your body. Exhale send it up into the sky.

Inhale the moonlight into your body. Exhale send it back down into the earth.

When you are finished give thanks to the Moon and the earth below you for providing their cleansing energy to you during this time.

Gemini – Self-Love

The sign with two faces provides us with many unique perspectives on life. The air element of Gemini is strongly connected with the mind. If you listen to your mind, you may notice that there is a critical voice and a kind voice. On the Full Moon, you may feel as though these two voices are heightened. It is important to listen to the words, tone, and encouragement of each voice. Notice which one is louder, or which one is more persuasive. If the voice of love is not the loudest, then this is the perfect ritual for you. If your voice of love is the loudest, this is a wonderful self-love reminder for you!

For this ritual, you will need:

- 2 pieces of paper
- A pen to write

- A quiet space to sit and listen to your thoughts

On the evening of the Full Moon, find a quiet space to listen to your thoughts. Sit in silence for a few minutes as you begin to observe the chatter of your mind. Listen to the voice of your mind that is kind, caring and loving toward you - we will call this the 'empowered mind'. Also, listen to the voice of the mind that is judgemental and focused on the negative things – we will call this the 'fearful mind'.

Once you have identified the difference between the two voices, take it to the paper.

On one piece of paper, write the words coming from the fearful mind. Feel the words as they are written on the paper; what do the words of fear do to your mind and body?

Tune into the positive mind now, even if it is not as loud, and listen to its whispers of encouragement. On the other piece of paper, write down these words of empowerment. The 'you can do it' phrases and expressions that this mind expresses.

You may find yourself swapping regularly between the two papers, as a negative thought pops in amongst the positive, or vice versa. Write it all down so that you can observe your mind from the outside. The mind works pretty quickly, so write until the pages are full.

When both pieces of paper are full, compare the words written on them both. Which words do you want to be the guiding force through the rest of your life?

Take the words of the fearful mind and rip the page up into small pieces. Take it to a place where you can bury it deep in the earth. Perhaps a place in your garden, or somewhere in nature. Make sure the paper is small enough so that it will decompose easily, allowing your fears to dissolve more quickly!

Take the notes of the empowered self and hang it up somewhere you see it regularly, perhaps on a mirror in your home, or next to your bed. Whenever you see this list, read some of the empowered words out loud to yourself, and feel the love speaking to you!

Cancer – Nature Swim

Cancer the crab is a water sign that feels comfortable in the depths of the oceans and lakes. On the Full Moon, a wonderful way to cleanse and release old energy is through immersing yourself in a body of water. This takes away old energy and leaves you feeling refreshed!

For this ritual, you will need:

- A body of water in nature (ocean, lake, waterfall, river etc)
- Your wild imagination

Set an intention for yourself to spend this Cancer Full Moon by a body of water. You can either spend an hour or a whole day by this water source that you choose, depending on how much time you have to relax.

Please note: If you do not live near any natural water source, you can choose a light river to simply dip your feet into, or alternatively, choose a swimming pool, or put some cold water in a bathtub, or a large bucket (big enough to stand in).

Before you head straight into the water, think about what it is you would like to let go of during this Full Moon. What emotion or feeling has been coming up for you that no longer serves a purpose? What lessons have you learnt and are ready to release?

Once you have that in mind, connect this feeling (or multiple feelings) with a colour (or multiple colours). Where does it live in your body? What does it look like? What does it feel like being stored within your body and mind?

Now head for the water, one of the most powerful cleansers of all. As you step into the water, feel the coolness of it wash around your feet. Feel the splashes of water playing with your ankles. If you can, submerge your feet fully.

As you stand here, imagine that the colour you chose for your emotion is now moving out of your feet and into the water. Using your powerful imagination, see that the water colour changes, your chosen colour pooling at your feet. This is the old energy moving out of you.

If you have the chance to walk deeper into the water, maybe you will feel this colour coming out of more parts of your body. Feel it leaving your body completely, and with the colour moving out, so too does the connected emotion. Breathe deeply as you submerge yourself in your chosen water wild water source.

If you cannot go deeper into the water, simply feel the colour at your feet. Take a few deep breaths here as the old energy leaves your body. When you feel that it has all been extracted, step out of the water, emerging as a new person – lighter and freer.

If your chosen water source is in nature, it will automatically transmute and change into clean pure water again, as does everything that flows with the natural cycles of nature. You can simply relax by the waterside now.

If your chosen water source was a bucket or bathtub, drain the water, or tip the contents of the bucket outside in nature so that the natural healing of nature can take care of it.

Finish off with three deep breaths, allowing your newfound sense of lightness to move around your body.

Leo – Candlelight Bathing

The fiery nature of Leo likes to stand out in a crowd, and what better way to stand out than to surround yourself with burning flames? Leo can comfortably sit in the centre of attention, all eyes on them, and fire is like fuel to a Leo so this potent combination will be used during this ritual.

For this ritual, you will need:

- At least twelve candles (these can be tealight candles or larger candles) – the more you have the better
- Matches or firelighter
- A safe space indoors or outdoors to burn the candles
- A comfortable seat, either cosy on the floor with cushions and blankets or on a chair

On the evening of the Full Moon, choose a comfortable location to sit, either indoors or outdoors. Make sure this space is safe for burning candles. Once you have set up a comfortable place to sit, create a circle of candles all around you. If you are using twelve candles, space them apart evenly to surround you. If you have more, then perhaps you can create a connected ring of fire around you. The candles do not need to be the same size or shape, it's the fire that is more important.

Please note: Do take fire precautions, perhaps putting each candle on a plate so that it doesn't burn the floor beneath you. Also, keep a bottle of water around in case you need to extinguish a flame!

Okay, now safety is out of the way, the fun can begin. Step into your circle with your matches or firelighter and stand in the middle. You are going to light each candle one by one, setting an intention for each candle. The intention will begin with the words:

May the light of your flame burn away ....
(Then you can fill in the blank - for example, use the words: fear, hopelessness, stress, pain, doubts etc.) You can ask each candle to burn away something different, or you can double up if you want extra help burning one thing away!

Once you have set an intention for each candle and they have all been lit, take your seat in the middle. Close your eyes and breathe deeply. Feel the gentle warmth coming from the candles around you.

Even with your eyes closed, do you see the shadows of the flickering light from behind your eyelids?

Enjoy bathing in this candlelight for around 15 to 20 minutes, but of course longer if you wish. As you rest here, feel that all your fears or worries are illuminated by the light of the candle, and are being burnt away by the flames. This self-held ceremony is one to let go of all that you no longer need, and to fill yourself with the warmth and beautiful light of the candles.

Here, under the Full Moon, all that you are is fully illuminated. Bathe in your delightful essence as you embrace the wild and wonderful energy of Leo.

Virgo – Smudging Ritual

Virgo energy is deeply connected with the earth. It is Virgo who is the wisdom keeper of the plant and animal kingdoms, sharing her gentle and caring energy with other living beings. Through communicating with plant spirits, she can utilise the plant energies for a cleansing ritual on the night of the Full Moon.

For this ritual, you can make your own equipment, if you so wish to. You will need a smudge stick, and if you decide to make this yourself, you will need to do so two weeks beforehand, during the New Moon!

If you want to create your own smudge stick, this ritual may require some planning. To do this, you can pick the plants on the New Moon, bundle them up and then let them dry for two weeks, ready to burn on the Full Moon.

Some plants you can use for smudging are pine trees, birch leaves, rose petals, rosemary, lavender, sage, or anything else growing in your local environment. When collecting plants, be sure to ask the plant spirit for permission first, and only take what is needed.

Once you have collected your plants, use a thin twine to bundle them up tightly into a 'smudge stick' shape – like a wand! Hang this bundle in a dry room and leave for one to two weeks in the lead-up to the Full Moon.

Alternatively, you can purchase one made by someone else if you would prefer.

On the evening of the Full Moon, you will need:

- Your own home-made smudge stick, or one you have purchased
- A candle and firelighter
- Space outdoors to smudge (or indoors but it will get smokey)

On the evening of the Full Moon, take your smudge stick, candle, and lighter and prepare your smudging space. Light the candle, calling in the fire spirit, and set it down.

Take your smudge stick in your hands and say the following aloud:

I call upon the spirits of "(use the names of the plants you used in your bundle)" to be here with me now, and to assist me in this cleansing ritual.

Take three deep breaths, allowing space and time for the plant spirits to arrive.

When you are ready, place the end of the smudge stick over the flame of the fire and light it. Blow out the flame, and allow the smoke of the plants to travel through the room or space you are in. Holding the smudge stick in your hand, wave it over your head, your heart, and your belly. You can re-light it if the smoke stops, repeating this as you move the wand through your entire energetic body field.

Feel the weight of the smoke carrying away the old energy, leaving you lighter. You will know when it feels right to stop, and at this point, put the smudge stick down.

As the smoke clears, see a vision of yourself lighter and brighter than before. This is the vision of your true self, the one you are walking towards becoming.

Let the smoke clear your path so that you can step up into the best version of yourself as you move forward from this Full Moon!

Libra – Balancing with Breath

Libra is all about balance, and what better way to balance the body than connecting with the breath? Libra is also related to the element of 'air', making breathwork practice the perfect ritual for a Libra Full Moon.

For this ritual, you will need:

- Yourself
- Your breath
- Space (preferably outside so that the air is fresh)

This ritual will use a specific way of breathing that has been used for thousands of years as an ancient yogic technique. It is known as *Nadi Shodana*, a Sanskrit word which roughly translates to 'cleansing the energy channels of your body'.

In a space where you can relax, find a comfortable seated position either on the floor, in nature, or on a chair. Straighten your spine, growing the crown of your head tall toward the sky and root your hips down into the earth. Take a deep breath through your nose and then exhale out through your mouth, arriving fully in the present moment.

Now, relax your left hand in your lap. Take your right hand to hover in front of your face. Connect your right pointer finger and middle finger to the space between your eyebrows. Take the right thumb to rest just outside of your right nostril and take your fourth finger to rest outside of the left nostril.

To practice alternate nostril breathing, follow these steps:

1. Press the fourth finger into the left nostril to block the airflow. Then inhale, drawing air in through the right nostril.

2. Hold your breath at the top for a moment. Release your fourth finger and press the thumb into your right nostril. Exhale through the left nostril.

3. Stay as you are and inhale through the left nostril. Then at the top of your breath, swap your fingers, release your thumb and press the fourth finger into the nostril, breathe out through the right nostril.

4. Repeat this cycle at least ten times. One full round of breathing is: *in through the right and out through the left, then in through the left and out through the right.*

At the end of this, release your hands into your lap and relax the breath. Notice if anything has changed in your mind or your body.

Do you feel the extra space that you have created in your lungs and body?

Enjoy the sensation of expansion and lightness as you carry these feelings under the light of the Full Moon.

Scorpio – Moonlight Meditation

During a Scorpio Moon, you can allow the deepest desires and secrets of your soul to surface to remind yourself of what you truly want in this lifetime. Scorpio usually likes to keep these aspects hidden, thinking that it is too much for the world to handle, but in fact, bringing the darkness to the light can result in deep healing and can help you to work toward these dreams.

For this ritual, you will need:

- A space to rest under the Full Moon
- A journal and pen to record any insights
- A blanket or two, and warm socks

Lay down somewhere comfortable, either on your bed, a couch, or a yoga mat and cover yourself with a blanket. Make sure you are warm, using extra blankets and warm socks if the weather is cool. The more comfortable you are, the easier it will be to surrender, completely relaxing every muscle in your body, and softening into the surface beneath you.

Close your eyes and gently connect with your breath. Imagine the light of the Full Moon above you, shining down on all parts of your body. As you gently scan through your body, imagine the Full Moon illuminating that specific area, like a bright torch shining on your body. Move really slowly, taking time to listen to each part of your body and what it wants to communicate.

In some parts of your body, you may notice there are hidden messages for you. For example, the belly might highlight your 'gut feeling' about a certain situation. Your heart may have a gentle wish that it wants you to hear. Perhaps a pain or injury in your body can speak to you more clearly under the light of the Full Moon. Listen deeply to the whispers of your body, as they unravel your secrets. The longer you listen, the more you may hear.

When you feel tuned in to your body and intuition, ask yourself these questions:

1. *What is my greatest wish that I have been hiding from the world?*
2. *What true part of myself am I hiding from others?*
3. *What messages from my body want to be illuminated under the light of this Full Moon?*

Imagine the moonlight pulling out these answers, bringing them up to the surface and into the open.

Rest here for as long as you feel called to.

When you are ready, gently open your eyes, turn to your journal and write about your insights. Perhaps also think of the next steps you need to take to bring your greatest wish into the world. Let your intuition guide your journaling and you may find new solutions that you didn't know were previously possible. Enjoy the mystery and messages that arise under this Scorpio Moon.

Sagittarius – Shaking Meditation

The fire sign Sagittarius likes to move! This means physically moving around the world, travelling, exploring and not being bound to one place. To embody a little bit of this energy on the Full Moon, you are invited to shake your body!

For this ritual, you will need:

- Epic music
- Headphones or a loud speaker
- A space where you feel free to move your body

Choose a song that makes your body move. Ideally, this song will have an upbeat pace, or deep rhythm that can make you forget about what's happening in the world around you.

Take three deep breaths to tune into what is happening in your body now. What is coming up for you with this Full Moon, and what wants to be shaken out of the body?

Put headphones in or if you are in a place where you can blast the music – blast it out loud!

Turn the music up and let the rhythm move your body.

Start by connecting with a shaking sensation, shaking the arms, the legs and the entire body, to move old energy out of your system. This can be like flicking the wrists and arms or bouncing up and down slightly, allowing the entire body to naturally move. Even if it feels a little funny at first, try to stick with it. Eventually, your mind will let go and your body will take over, shaking and moving you naturally.

Keep shaking for at least three minutes, but if you want to keep going for longer, then keep going until you feel like it's time to stop. You may also notice that your shaking transitions into more of a dance style and that's okay too! Keep the playlist rolling and let your body move however it wants to.

When the music has come to an end, sit down on the floor in stillness. Close your eyes. Put one hand on your heart, one on your belly. Feel the creative fire you have ignited within you. Feel the blood pumping around your body. That powerful energy that moves within you is your life force. It's the ideas, inspiration, and love that move around your body freely.

As you enjoy this new energy in your body, ask yourself these questions:

1. What has changed or shifted in your body or mind since you started moving and shaking?

2. What space have you created within you by vibrating the old energy cells out of your body?

3. Where is your creative life force (the ideas, inspiration and love) guiding you next?

Capricorn – Leaning into Surrender

Capricorn is a planner. They are the ones who like to have all the little details sorted so that they can enjoy their holiday. Or the one that already knows exactly what they will do in a day, planned hour for hour. One of the challenges of Capricorn is letting go of the planning and trusting in the bigger plan at play. This is what you will get to explore in this ritual.

For this ritual, you will need:

- To let go of your previous plan
- To trust in the unknown
- An open and excited mind
- Around two to four hours of time

On the day of the Full Moon, set aside a couple of hours to try something new. Take yourself out of the house and to a new town, shopping mall, place in nature, or event of your choice. Preferably this will be a place that you have never been before, as this will ensure that you need to make spontaneous decisions without knowing the likely outcome.

When you are at the chosen place, ask yourself: which direction should I walk? Trust the first insight that comes to you. You may hear a quick message in your mind, or a sensation of a gut feeling. Whatever it is, let your intuition guide you in the right direction.

If you are in nature, you might find that this leads you to a new place, a special lookout, or a river to jump into! At every turn or place you find – consult your intuition. For example: *Should I jump in that river?* Listen to the first answer that comes.

If you are in a shopping mall, listen to what shops your intuition guides you toward. Maybe you find a special gift for yourself to remind you of this day, or maybe you find a delicious scoop of ice cream in your hand.

Whatever you do, it should be totally unplanned, spontaneous and in a new location. This will keep the surprise element alive and in action. Don't forget to keep in touch with your intuition (which may be a little harder in a shopping mall than in nature due to the advertising and loud noises all around). Either way, if this inner force guides you, you may realise that it created more opportunities than could have ever been seen if the day was totally pre-planned.

Pre-planning is not always a bad idea, indeed it can be helpful sometimes, but the beauty is in the balance of plans and spontaneity for a real adventure to unfold!

Enjoy the surprises that come your way on this Full Moon day.

Aquarius – Chakra Connection

Aquarius is the sign of the future, the one who is comfortable playing around with new energies and creating futuristic ideas. For this ritual, you will transcend the physical body and instead, connect with your energy body. This is the energy body that is influenced by the Full Moon.

For this ritual, you will need:

- A space to relax
- A creative imagination
- A journal and pen

Begin by finding a comfortable seated position, using pillows or blankets to support your body if you need them.

The chakras are spinning energy centres in your body. Each chakra holds a different energy and is represented by a different colour. As you connect with each centre today under the Full Moon, feel the message that each one has for you. You can ask the following questions in your mind, or you can write about your answer in your journal.

Root Chakra – located at the very base of your spine. Connect with the colour red in your mind's eye. The energy here makes you feel grounded, supported and safe.

Connection Question: *How can I connect more with my physical body?*

Sacral Chakra – located beneath the navel. Connect with the colour orange in your mind's eye. The energy here makes you feel creative, expressive, and connected with your sexuality.

Connection Question: *Where can I invite more creativity into my life?*

Solar Plexus Chakra – located just above the navel. Connect with the colour yellow in your mind's eye. The energy here makes you feel powerful, planned, and purposeful.

Connection Question: *Where do I need to step into a place of power in my life?*

Heart Chakra – located in the centre of the chest. Connect with the colour green in your mind's eye. The energy here makes you feel joyful, compassionate, and loving.

Connection Question: *How can I move with love through my life?*

Throat Chakra – located in the centre of the neck. Connect with the colour blue in your mind's eye. The energy here makes you feel as though you want to speak your truth, speak up for yourself and others in need, and express clarity in your words.

Connection Question: *Where do I need to voice my opinion or express myself more clearly?*

Third Eye Chakra – located in the centre of the forehead between the two eyebrows. Connect with the colour indigo in your mind's eye. The energy here makes you feel intuitive, inspired, and in tune with your clear vision of the future.

Connection Question: *What vision of the future do I see for myself?*

Crown Chakra – located on top of the head, in the centre. Connect with the colour white in your mind's eye. The energy here makes you feel connected, energetic, and as that we are all one.

Connection Question: *Am I connected with a higher power?*

Carry these answers with you, and enjoy the clarity that they have bought to you on this Full Moon day.

Pisces – Moon water

As the ruler of the deep blue oceans, Pisces is no stranger to the qualities of water. In particular, this sign knows how to connect deeply with the spiritual side of water, and to create a unique essence of its own. You can try this yourself in this ritual.

For this ritual, you will need:

- A glass of water
- A small plate
- Crystals (if you have some)
- Herbs, flowers, or edible plants (preferably loose leaf, but an herbal tea bag will also work)

To begin, fill a glass with pure, clean, filtered water.

Choose a number of herbs, crystals, flowers or plants that are safe to consume. You may find these out in the garden, in the wild, or in your kitchen. Each thing that you choose should represent something to you. For example, rose petals may represent the opening up of the heart. A clear quartz crystal may represent new energy in your life. Whatever it is, pick it with intention and give it a meaning. These are the things that will be infused into your Moon water.

One by one, place them in your glass of water with the intention you have chosen.

Please note: If you are not sure whether or not a foraged herb or crystal is safe to consume, simply place it beside the glass to infuse energetically.

Set this glass out under the moonlight, maybe on a windowsill, or outdoors and leave it to sit overnight. Cover it with a small plate to ensure nothing gets in overnight and then leave the water to rest. It will soak up the energy of your chosen plants and crystals and infuse this into your water.

When you rise in the morning, first thing upon waking, drink your glass of Moon water. Reconnect with the intentions that you set with each herb, crystal or plant and feel these intentions filling your body and cells. Your glass is also infused with full moonlight now too, so feel this nourishing your inner body and shining its bright light from within.

As you move about the rest of your day, let your intentions and moonlight shine out of you, into the world around you!

As you move through each Full Moon cycle, keep track of how these rituals play out in your life. If you journaled about a certain aspect that you wanted to let go of, then check back into that journal entry three or six months later. By looking back, you will see if you truly did let go of that old habit, situation, place or thing that you wanted to let go of. This is how you can keep track of progress and notice the difference that these rituals are making in your life!

When you see progress, you are also more likely to stay on track and keep working toward your long-term goals through the work of short-term cycles. This is what we are going to explore in the next chapter – manifesting with the Moon!

Chapter 8

Manifesting with the Moon

This chapter reinforces the power of using the Moon cycles and rituals together to manifest your dreams and desires. It is a topic that weaves its way in and out of this book, reminding you that ultimately, you can use the Moon as your personal power tool!

As we have explored throughout the last chapters, there is a strong and unique energy associated with each phase of the Moon and with each zodiac sign that is ruling the Moon at a certain time. By tapping into the specific energy that is present each month, you can charge up your dreams and wishes. The energy can be used for cleansing, clearing, paving a new path, and of course for manifestation.

What is Manifestation?

Manifestation sounds like a 'new-age' word that is thrown about all over the place. "Manifest what you want, call it into your life, live your dream!" Although it sounds easy and quick on the outside, the inner use of manifestation takes time, intention, and the focus of your energy.

Yes, manifestation is the idea and practice of bringing your future dreams and wishes into the present moment. But, this is done by aligning your thoughts with your actions. You can't just sit around and wish that your dreams will come true without even getting off the couch!

How to Manifest What You Truly Desire

To work with manifestation, you need to state clearly what you want to bring into your life. Although these can be physical items, the best manifestation comes when you connect with the emotional aspect of what you are bringing in.

For example, if you want to manifest a bigger house, ask yourself this: What emotions will you feel when you have a bigger house?

This could be the feeling of joy, spaciousness in day-to-day life, success, etc. These feelings are more important than the goal itself. If you connect with your feelings, you may find that other things can bring you these same sensations, bringing you closer to your goal step by step, and feeling supported by the Universe along the way.

So, are you ready to call in your dream life? Get clear on your answers to the following questions. Write them down, draw them up, and create some kind of concrete memory of what you are wishing for.

1. In your ideal life, how do you want to feel when you get out of bed each day?

2. What do you want your days to consist of? What activities, events, places, or people are present in your life? How do these things make you feel?

3. What do you want to feel each day within your mind and body? For example, more peacefulness, inner calm, inspiration, or motivation? Choose feelings that are unique to you and your current circumstances.

4. The final question: After a day filled with the things you love and some lessons learned, how do you want to feel when you put your head on the pillow to go to sleep? What is the final feeling in your heart, mind, and body at the end of the day?

To practice bringing the future into the present moment, feel this feeling of gratitude, contentment, or joy as you imagine resting your head on the pillow at the end of a wonderful day. What do these feelings do in your body now? Where does gratitude reside within you? What does contentment feel like? How does joy move through you?

As you connect with these feelings, you are consciously calling them into this very moment. This moment is all we truly have. So, by bringing the future into the moment of now, you are already shifting your energy and creating the new you!

Now, let's take it to the next level. Aside from the day-to-day life that you wish to live, think about what you really want to achieve in this lifetime.

To determine this, think about:

1. What are your overarching values that guide you through this life?

2. What does success look like for you?

3. What things do you want or not want to have in your life?

Once you have your ideal reality in your mind. Write it down to concretize it. You can use written words, but you can also use images, dreams, and strong emotions.

Now you've got clarity, it's time to link these goals up with the Moon cycles to harness the ultimate potential!

Every Moon cycle presents an opportunity that could help you to take a step toward this dream of yours. For example, if you implement a new habit during every New Moon, and let go of an old habit during every Full Moon, your life is going to be changing quickly.

We can break this down by looking at the difference between short-term and long-term manifesting.

Short-Term Manifesting – Working With the Moon Phases

Short-term manifesting can be practiced within one complete Moon cycle. This means you can set a goal and see it come to fruition in about twenty-nine days. Just as we spoke about the energy of the Moon phases, this manifestation starts on a New Moon, moves through a Full Moon, and reaches its culmination at the next New Moon.

This means working closely with the general energy of the phases that we discussed in Chapter Two.

To recap this for you:

Each New Moon is a time to set an intention for a new beginning. As the Moon grows, moving toward its full state, you can let the seed of intention grow too. At full illumination, use the energy to shed away anything that is holding you back as the Full Moon lights up the sky. Then, reflect and get ready to reset as the next New Moon comes around again.

For example, this could look like setting an intention to begin a new hobby or project at the time of the New Moon, and continue it for twenty-nine days, refining it and seeing how it unfolds during one Moon cycle. At the Full Moon, you may swap out an old habit that is holding you back from getting good at this new hobby – hello procrastination, it's time for you to go!

Another idea is that you could set an intention to clear out your home and simplify your living space. You could gather up items you no longer need and on the Full Moon donate them to a charity shop. This will clear space for what you want to try as the next Moon cycle rolls around.

This Moon cycle timeframe allows for a practical and achievable goal to be set and to be followed through. Month upon month, if you commit to bringing one new thing in, and letting one old thing go, things will start to change. Before you know it, your life will start to look very different as you move toward a new version of you!

Long-Term Manifesting – Working With the Ruling Zodiac Sign

For long-term manifesting, you'll be working with the specific energy of each ruling zodiac sign. To keep on track, it is ideal if you can take a yearly calendar and mark the dates of each New and Full Moon in your calendar, either digitally or written in a paper diary. As you write down each of the Moon phases, connect them with the relevant zodiac sign (you'll have to go back to Chapter Two for this). Working with the zodiac energy will give you an idea of which energy theme to work with at that specific time.

Once you've got the zodiac signs and the dates of the New and Full Moon in your calendar, take a separate journal or piece of paper, and think about a long-term goal that you want to achieve. This could be something like a new job, new house, new city, or new partner. It can help to imagine the person that you want to be this time next year. What is that person doing? What does your future look like?

What do you think you can achieve in twelve months? Even if it feels like a bit of a stretch to achieve it, write it down, as when you are supported by the Moon and the energy present all around you, big changes can happen fast!

Now, when your goal is clear, split that big goal into smaller pieces to make it more achievable. This means, breaking it down into twelve digestible goals that don't feel too overwhelming (note: this is short-term manifesting).

The next step is to connect each 'short-term' goal with each Moon cycle, using the specific energy of the zodiac to support you. You may need to reflect back on the rituals in Chapters Five and Seven to recall the specific energy of each zodiac sign. While you're at it, it's also a great time to schedule your rituals with your manifestation goals too!

Once you understand the zodiac energy, you can connect it with a corresponding goal.

For example, if you need to make a big physical change, do it during a fire sign transit – either Leo, Aries, or Sagittarius Moons. If you need to make a more subtle personality change or tap into your emotions more, choose to set this goal during a water sign transit – either Cancer, Scorpio, or Pisces Moons. Organizational tasks and planning are best done during an earth sign transit – either Capricorn, Taurus, or Virgo Moons. More sociable goals and plans to network with others are best done during air sign transits – either Gemini, Aquarius, or Libra Moons.

By connecting the goals with the right energy, the Moon itself will help you to stay true to your goal, because with collective energy, all people on Earth will be affected by the same energy of the Moon transit at that time!

Go with the Flow

Remember, your goals can shift or even change completely during the year, and that's okay! Reconnect with your overarching values, alter your goals so you are still on track, and then utilize the energy of the Moon to replan and organize your next steps. Just as energy is always in motion, so too are our thoughts, feelings, and goals. By allowing your dreams to unfold naturally, more magic will occur than you ever thought would be possible!

Working with the Moon should not feel like a chore, but it should feel practical and easily be implemented into your daily life. The more familiar you become with the Moon phases and zodiac signs, the easier it will be to make this form of manifestation part of your everyday life.

Although the beginning of this Moon phase journey may involve a little study and effort to stay on track, this will be replaced with awe and motivation as the lessons start to become a part of your reality. Soon, you will embody the energy of the Moon, and feel that the knowledge is stored deep within your bones. You will live and breathe with the cycles of the Moon, and you'll be totally present as you swim through the cosmic energy of the zodiac signs. When this time comes, naturally, and without extreme effort, the results of your manifestations will start to become evident in your life.

Trusting the Signs – How Do You Know the Manifesting is Working?

There is a big part of the Universe, the Moon, the Sun, and all the planets, that want to see you achieve the dreams and wishes that you set out to create. As you consciously bring Moon cycle work into your life, you may notice little (or large) signs of support from the Universe. This can come in many forms or signs, so let's break it down and find out what a 'sign' really is.

A sign is something that you will recognize as a familiar reminder that you are on the right path. It can come in many ways, but it always feels like it is delivered in divine timing. Often, you may brush these 'signs' off as sheer coincidence, but just for a moment, if you could believe that there is no such thing as coincidence, then perhaps you would be open to accepting it as a sign from the Universe.

For example, a sign may be a text message from a friend that is received at the same time you were thinking of them. It could also be a passing message from a stranger on the street, a visit from a spirit animal, or a message that you received in nature. It could be a spontaneous invitation to an event where there is someone to meet who could help you with your project. Or it could be that a feather falls from the sky, landing at your feet, just at the moment you were thinking of your future. This could be a sign that you are on the right track toward that dream.

These signs are the way that the energy of the Moon confirms that you are on the right track. They may seem random, out of place, or even uncanny, but you will have a gut feeling that this is a form of communication from the Universe when these signs come your way.

By following the guidance of these signs, trusting your own intuition, and walking on your path of truth, you will be building the life of your dreams, day by day, week by week. After a year has gone by, you can reflect back on your calendar and witness the changes that you made to your life. This is when you will know that the power of manifestation is working with you in every choice you make.

Chapter 9

Special Moon Phases

By this stage, I'm sure you're familiar with the general waxing and waning of the Moon, the different energy between the New and the Full Moon, and you also know how to connect the phases with the zodiac signs, right? You've got the basics covered and you are ready to apply these learnings to your own life. But in this final chapter, we will explore one more unique factor that also contributes to the energy of the Moon. These are called the 'special' Moon phases.

Special? What can be more special than a big, bright, Full Moon, you ask? A Supermoon! Or perhaps a Supermoon eclipse. Let's look into the eclipse portals, Blood Moons, Micromoons, and more... are you ready to expand your knowledge once again?

What is a Special Moon Phase?

A special Moon is a type of Moon that does not occur regularly, or even according to a certain pattern, but is a special and unique phenomenon in the sky. The special Moons that we will look at here are Supermoons, eclipses, Blood Moon, Harvest Moon, and Micromoons. Each one occurs for its own specific reason, and at a specific time too (which can sometimes feel random as it's not necessarily a linear pattern).

Just as the normal Moon phases hold a special energy, so too do these special Moons. Whether they hold extra manifestation powers, uncover more of your shadows, or have the ability to pull more emotions out of you, each one is worth knowing about.

It is also a great idea to find out which Moons are influenced by these special phases and add it to your Moon calendar so you can track when the energy is going to be a little more challenging, or perhaps a little more powerful than your average Full Moon. Let's start with Supermoons!

Supermoons

A Supermoon occurs when the Moon is located at its closest proximity to Earth during its orbit. Although the Super Full Moons gather the most attention because they are seen shining brightly in the sky, a Supermoon can actually happen during any Moon phase. Yes, even including New Moons. Even though you won't see a Super New Moon in the sky, you will still feel its effect energetically.

A Super Full Moon creates a larger-looking Moon in the sky. Although it is only slightly larger than the average Full Moon, the difference is big enough to bring extra energy into our bodies and the world around us. This means that during a Supermoon, the energy can be more potent than usual, and it may exaggerate the qualities of the zodiac sign that the Moon is in.

What Should You Do During a Supermoon?

If you feel like electricity is running through your veins during a Supermoon, it's time to ground down. Use the rituals provided in the previous chapters to reconnect with your body. Put your bare feet on the earth, lay on a patch of grass, and take time out for a few deep breaths. Try to move slowly and with caution during a Supermoon transit.

How Often Do Supermoons Occur?

Supermoons occur around three to four times a year, either at a New or Full Moon phase. Sometimes, they can even occur more frequently.

Why Is It Called a Supermoon?

The term 'Supermoon' was created in 1979 by astrologer Richard Nolle, who observed the phenomenon of the 'extra-large sized Moon' in the sky. Since then, some astrologers have seen Supermoons coincide with natural disasters, such as earthquakes or hurricanes. Perhaps you can start to track this too as you spend more time Moon gazing and following the cycles.

Eclipses

A lunar eclipse can only occur when it is a Full Moon, and at the same time, the Moon is near to a lunar node. This means that the Sun, Moon, and Earth will align in a straight line. Due to the Moon's proximity to the lunar nodes during an eclipse, it plays a significant role in astrology. If you go back to the basics of astrology, you may remember that the two lunar nodes that you will find on your birth chart (north and south) represent the 'past' and the 'future' you. This means that during an eclipse, either your past or future self will be activated, bringing up old lessons or future skills that you may need to work with at this time.

What Should You Do During an Eclipse?

During an eclipse season, a potent portal of transformation opens. When an eclipse portal opens it highlights everyone's personal journey from who they are (or have been) to who they are becoming. This means moving from the past (south node) to the future (north node). These portals can be somewhat of an unpredictable time, creating many surprises!

During this time, think about the best possible version of yourself. Work with the portal energy to think about how will you get there, to that future version of yourself. If you focus on mapping out your direction from past to future at this time, you might find that signs and synchronicities appear to help you jump forward into the next stage of being.

How Often Do Eclipses Occur?

You have to be on the night side of the Earth to see a lunar eclipse, and if you have to chance to witness it from your location, you don't want to miss it. On average, a total lunar eclipse can be seen from any given location every 2.5 years.

Although partial lunar eclipses may occur during Full Moon phases, only about 29% of all lunar eclipses are total lunar eclipses.

In astrology, there is a well-known 'eclipse season' which happens approximately every six months. This is when the Earth aligns between the Moon and Sun, and due to the rotational speed of the planets. This period of eclipses lasts around 34.5 days, creating an eclipse on each Full Moon that shines during this time.

Why Is It Called an Eclipse?

Eclipse means, 'the total or partial obscuring of one celestial body by another'. This is exactly what happens during an eclipse, therefore the word was invented to describe this unique astrological phenomenon.

Blood Moons

A Blood Moon is a time when the Moon takes on a red glow. This red phenomenon in the sky is an unusual sight, and can sometimes feel unsettling.

What Should You Do During a Blood Moon?

The red hue of the Moon reminds us to tap into our physical bodies, the earth, and to embrace this special time. Guided by the energy of transformation in the eclipse portal, the Blood Moon is the reminder to take practical action. Yes, dreaming is good, but what is a dream if no action follows it?

During a Blood Moon, think about this: *What is the next right step for me to take?*

This will help to keep you on track as you move through this lunar transit.

How Often Do Blood Moons Occur?

The red Moon is seen most obviously during a total lunar eclipse of a Supermoon (refer to eclipses above!).

Although a Blood Moon may arise at other times and phases of an eclipse, you'll have to find out just how frequently that is for yourself by gazing at the sky. There is no set sequence or prediction of how often these occur.

Why Is It Called a Blood Moon?

A Blood Moon gets its name from the red glow that it emits as it shines in the night sky. This phenomenon occurs during a total lunar eclipse, when the Earth moves directly between the Moon and the Sun, blocking the Sun's light from reaching the Moon's surface. The light that does reach the Moon is only from the shadows of the Earth, creating a blood-like colour.

Harvest Moons

The Harvest Moon is a Full Moon that occurs during the harvesting season, once a year. It usually rises soon after sunset, providing extra light long into the evening. Although it is traditionally related to the work of farmers on their land, this time can be celebrated by everyone as you reap the rewards of your efforts from the previous weeks or months. It is a transformative time, but also deeply nurturing for the mind, body, and spirit.

What Should You Do During a Harvest Moon?

Harvest something! This is a time of celebrating the harvest and the abundance of life. See what is on offer in your part of the world, and harvest a fruit, vegetable, or flower to celebrate this time of abundance.

It's also a wonderful time to count your blessings. What are you grateful for this year? What goals have you already grown and harvested? Reflect and celebrate the achievements of both yourself and your loved ones.

How Often Do Harvest Moons Occur?

The Harvest Moon is a once-a-year Moon. It is the Full Moon that occurs closest to the time of the Autumn Equinox in the Northern Hemisphere. This is usually in September or October.

Why Is It Called a Harvest Moon?

This Full Moon traditionally falls during the Harvest season, therefore named a Harvest Moon! It was celebrated as it provided extra light in the sky for working extra hours when the crop was ready to be harvested.

Micromoons

A Micromoon (or Mini Moon) is the opposite of a Supermoon. These Moons occur when the Moon is furthest away from the Earth, making the Moon appear small in the sky! This means to classify as a Micromoon, the center of the Moon must be further than 405,000 km away from the center of the Earth. Now, that's a long way!

In comparison, a Supermoon happens when the Moon is less than 360,000km from Earth. Making a 45,000 km difference between Supermoons and Micromoons.

What Should You Do During a Micromoon?

This is a good time to zoom out and see your life from a new perspective. Look from the distance at the things you seem to be getting caught up in. Is an issue at work taking up all your energy? Is a past event holding you back from achieving something new? Use the Micromoon energy to look at these types of situations from a bird's eye view. Will this matter in a year? In ten years? If not, then let go of the little worries now and shift your attention to the big picture instead. During a Micromoon, don't let the little things hold you back!

How Often Do Micromoons Occur?

It takes 27.5 days for the Moon to move from its closest point to Earth to the furthest point away. This means that a Micromoon will occur 27.5 days after the Supermoon!

Why Is It Called a Micromoon?

As a result of Micromoons being further away from the Earth, the Moon will look 14% smaller than a Supermoon. There will also be less illumination of the Moon's surface, making it appear up to 30% smaller and often less bright.

Tracking The Energy of the Moon

These extra potent portals of energy are a way to fast-track what you're manifesting.

Keep an eye out on your favorite astrology sites to track when a special Moon Phase is coming up.

If you've got the energy of a Supermoon behind you, dream big! If it's a Micromoon, take a step back! If the Harvest Moon is here, celebrate all that you have an abundance of, and if the Blood Moon is shining, connect with your body and the earth.

When an eclipse portal opens up, walk through that energy knowing that your life will look different on the other side. The Moon creates this energy for change to support you on your vision and path toward the 'new you'! The 'you' that you are manifesting and dreaming of. It's time to make your dreams a reality.

Conclusion

As the Full Moon sets on the horizon, and the lunar rays fade as the Sun begins to rise, you are reminded of the lessons and the special moments that occurred during the last Moon cycle. As you contemplate the moments of presence you shared, connected with the Moon, you remember that every moment was a special one. When you choose to live a life in sync with the greater forces of the Universe, every moment is divinely aligned. By doing this work, hopefully, the greater purpose of your journey here on Earth becomes clearer and your motivation and passion rise to the surface.

Living in harmony with the Moon's phases is an instinct that resides within all of us. During this book, did you reignite that instinct as you moved through the rituals and engaged in the lunar energy? The more we trust our inner nature, the deeper our connection can be to the natural world.

Throughout these pages, you learned about the ancestral connections with the Moon, as well as understanding evidence about how the Moon affects nature's tidal changes and animal mating habits. Then you dived deep into the Moon phases and the specific energy associated with each phase. You also learned how to bring these phases into daily life to work with the power of manifestation and were provided with twenty-four lunar rituals to harness the energy of the New and Full Moons!

Each cycle is another round, another intention, another chance to let go and make space for the new ideas and inspiration that are wiggling their way into your life. Take this moment now to reflect on what has happened or changed in your life as a result of this book.

Did any major events occur? Did you change your outlook on life? Were you able to connect more deeply with the energy of the moon?

If you kept a journal during this time, now could be a good time to flick back through the pages and consciously remember which manifestations came to fruition. Reflection is always a good idea, especially when we need to remember and realign with the goals that we set earlier. It's a chance to keep moving forward in the direction of your dreams while new insights and inspiration flow your way.

If you found that this book had an impact on your life, think of someone else that you would like to share this wisdom with. Having an accountability buddy to keep you in check with your rituals and Moon-watching can make the experience even more fun! You can share insights and even partake in the rituals together.

Leaving a review online is another great way to help other people find the insights and access to information that you have just absorbed. What feels better than helping other people to rise to their highest potential? If you enjoyed the content of this book, please, take one quick minute to leave a review. Let's help humanity to grow together! The more Moon gazers there are in the world, the easier it will be to move forward to a new era of lunar manifestation magic!

Remember, keep working with this book, and return to it each New and Full Moon to complete one of the rituals! You should also set alarms in your phone calendar or written reminders in your diary, to prepare and move through the Moon energy with ease.

Before you close the pages of this book, just for a short moment, imagine this...

You fast forward to meet the future version of yourself. In this vision, you are deeply connected with the Moon cycles, and you watch the Moon through its phases, fascinated by the magic it is creating in your life. You whisper to the Moon, and it whispers back, telling you of the energy that is being emitted to work with. You feel confident participating in lunar rituals, and you make time each month to celebrate and embrace the teachings of the Moon cycles. You find that life is going your way and things come to you with ease. Everything simply flows. You know that you put in the effort that it took to get here, to really embody this ancient wisdom, and now you can see the positive changes that have occurred in your life. You make proactive choices each day to work with the Moon, rather than against it, and in doing so, you have created the life of your dreams.

Take a deep breath in, holding this vision in your mind, noticing how it feels in your body. Bring a gentle smile to your face, knowing that you are already on your way to being this version of yourself. Then let out a soft breath, settling down and relaxing. Feel the lunar light in every cell of your body.

Although this book has come to a physical end, the energy lives on. It is an energy that can be returned to monthly, or even daily as you find the part of the cycle that you are currently connected with. As energy moves forward, changes are made, and you step into your full magnetic power. You are reminded that the cycle continues again and again, through this lifetime and the next...

Leave a Review Here

Scan the QR code below to leave your review on Amazon

About the Author

Ashley was born in a little village just outside of Ojai, California.

She grew up surrounded by open-minded people, like her mother, who worked as a herbalist for the majority of her life. Ever since she was little, Ashley watched her mom skilfully investigate the planetary connections of plants, and understand the alignment of plants with individuals' birth charts. She learnt from a young age the powerful role that astrology and botany have in healing others.

Ashley has always been fascinated by her mother's work, joining many 'witch circles' with her mom to learn more about the ancient art.

After finishing her 5-year long degree in Naturopathy, Ashley attended many courses about astrology, human design, crystals, and shamanic ways of healing.

She is deeply passionate about helping others achieve clarity about themselves. She often says that astrology has supported her throughout her entire life and been the driving force which helped her surpass her struggles and reach peace.

Since achieving her own inner peace, Ashley has used her knowledge and experiences to help many others across the globe to understand their own personalities, to find their perfect lovers, to attract financial abundance and to, essentially, find their *true* purpose!

In this book, Ashley has aimed to give readers just a small taste of the vast amount of knowledge she has on the subject of Astrology. She wants this book to be the start of an ongoing awakening for all and truly hopes that her writing speaks to the souls of all who read it!

ALSO WRITTEN BY ASHLEY BRITTANY

Discover the enchanting world of astrology with "*Astrology for Beginners: A Guide to Understanding Your Birth Chart, Star Sign, and Ideal Relationship Partner*", the captivating first book in the astrology series by the talented Ashley Brittany.

As you delve into the cosmic tapestry of zodiac signs, planetary influences, and celestial secrets, prepare to be mesmerized by Ashley's insightful wisdom and lyrical prose.

But the journey doesn't end here. If you are seeking empowerment, self-discovery, and a deeper connection with the universe, Ashley's book series is here to accompany you on this cosmic expedition.

Inspire the younger generation around you to ignite a passion for astrology with Ashley's second book, 'Astrology for Teens: A Guide to Understanding Yourself, Your Relationships, and Finding Your Place in the Universe'.

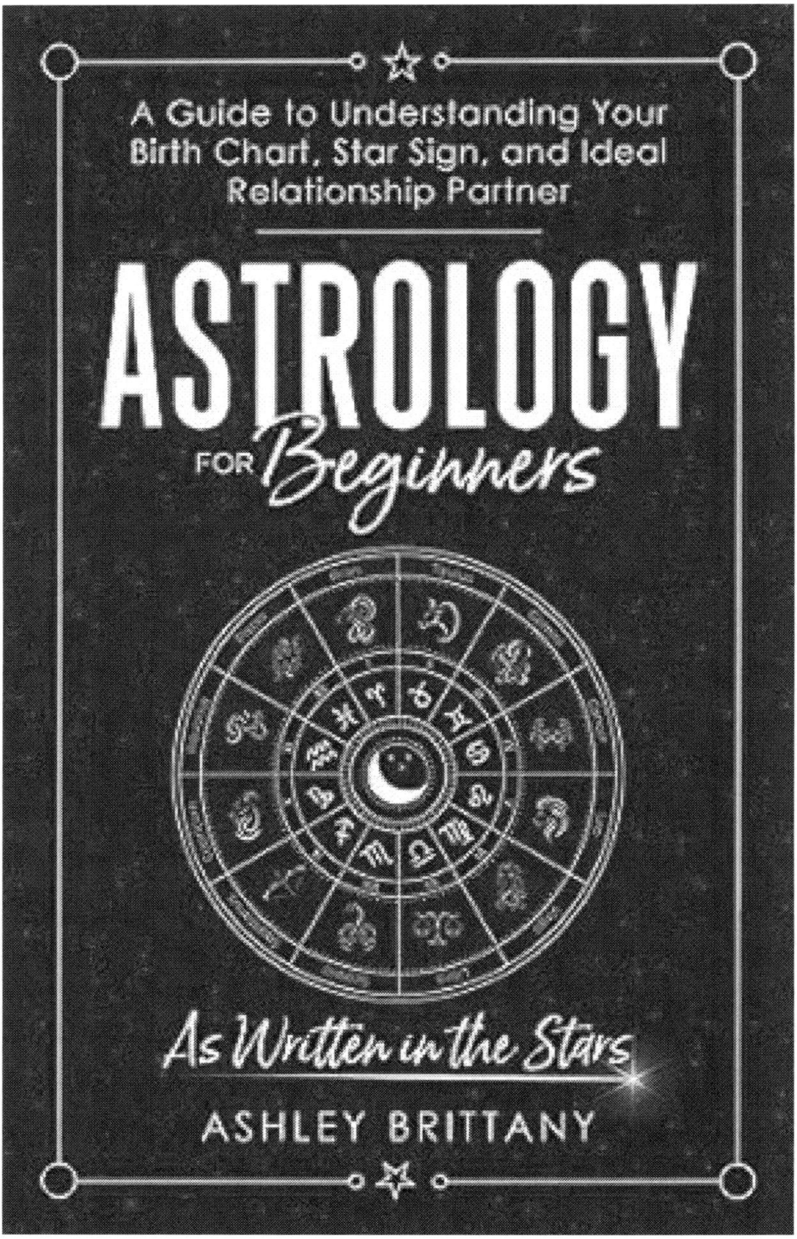
A Guide to Understanding Your Birth Chart, Star Sign, and Ideal Relationship Partner
ASTROLOGY
FOR Beginners
As Written in the Stars
ASHLEY BRITTANY

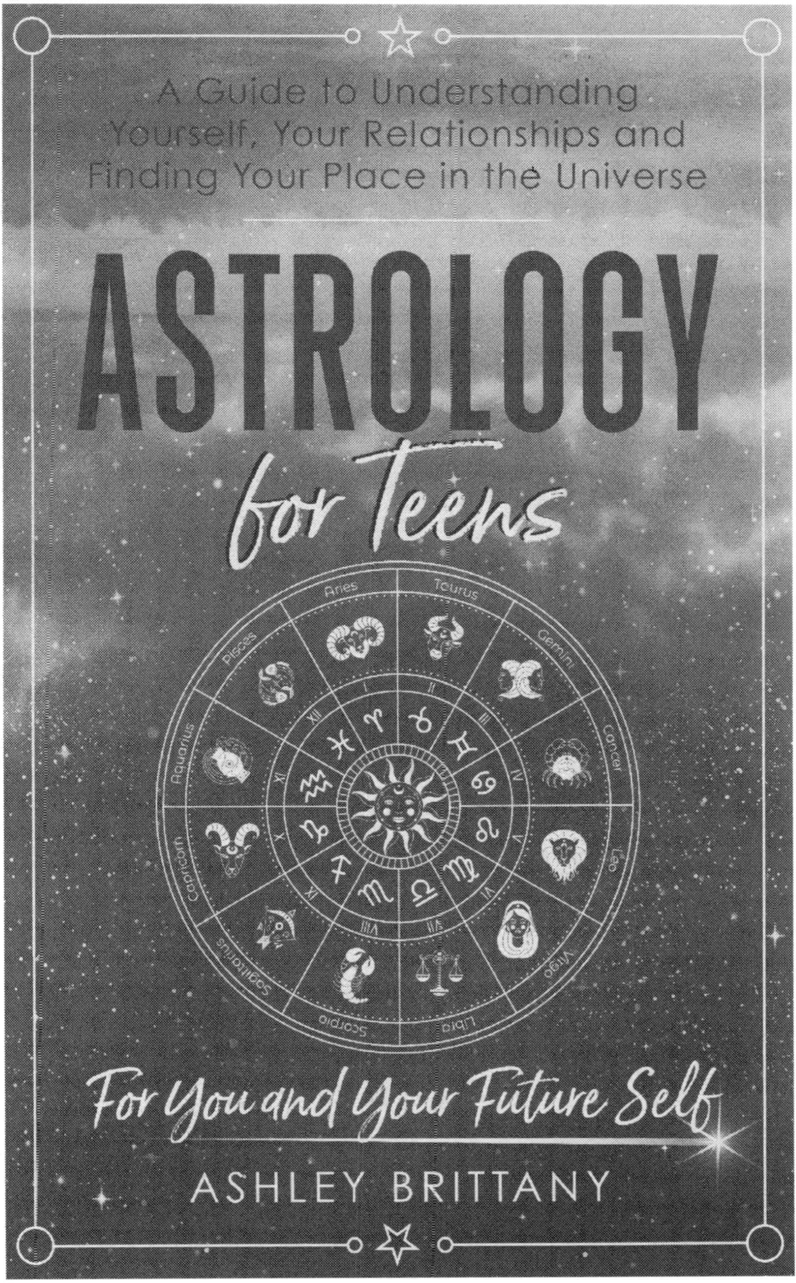
A Guide to Understanding Yourself, Your Relationships and Finding Your Place in the Universe
ASTROLOGY
for Teens
Aries
Taurus
Gemini
Cancer
Leo
Virgo
Libra
Scorpio
Sagittarius
Capricorn
Aquarius
Pisces
For You and Your Future Self
ASHLEY BRITTANY

Printed in Great Britain
by Amazon

5437b884-1f11-4e80-adc7-766617693754R01